WATERLOO
TO WEYMOUTH

WATERLOO
TO WEYMOUTH

A Journey in Steam

ANDREW BRITTON

First published 2014

The History Press
The Mill, Brimscombe Port
Stroud, Gloucestershire, GL5 2QG
www.thehistorypress.co.uk

British Library Cataloguing in Publication Data.
A catalogue record for this book is available from the British
Library.

ISBN 978 0 7524 9883 6

Typesetting and origination by The History Press
Printed in India

Cover illustrations: *Front*: Lord Nelson Class 30857 Lord Howe
at Basingstoke, 1962. *Back*: An Ivatt tank hauls the two-coach
Bulleid branch train across the Corfe viaduct, 1965. (Both Britton
Collection)

CONTENTS

ACKNOWLEDGEMENTS

I wish to extend my sincere thanks to the Her Majesty's Department of Transport & Industry, Network Rail and British Railways Board Archive for a major contribution to the production of this book as they have generously consented to the use of maps, diagrams and gradient details for inclusion. I have also purchased items in auctions and these authorities have generously consented to allow me to reproduce their redundant items, many now fifty years old or more.

I owe a great debt of thanks for photographic contributions to: Alan Sainty, Barry Eagles, John Cox, Bryan Hicks, Martin Robinson and David Peters. Without their considerable help, this book could not have been written.

As always my brother-in-law, Mike Pringle, has meticulously scanned and restored the slides and illustrations in this book. Additionally Mike has photographed the original diagrams. My sister, Ruth, has encouraged me immensely with this book, recalling long-forgotten facts and details. Their help has been invaluable.

One person who has monitored the progress of this book and proof-read the text is Michael Jakeman. He has once again proved to be invaluable with his sharp eye for detail and knowledge of railways.

I must say a big thank you to my wife Annette for supporting me on a daily basis when researching and writing this book, and also to my sons Jonathan, Mark and Matthew, and daughter-in-law Louise for all their help.

INTRODUCTION

This book describes Britain's last steam mainline from London and explores the train journey from Waterloo to Weymouth, plus the linked branch lines prior to the end of steam in 1967.

This fascinating journey is packed with rich historical and geographical detail and provides a wealth of information about the railway landscape between London and the south-coast legendary kingdom of Wessex, showing:

Gradients
Mileages
Speeds
Junctions
Viaducts and bridges
Tunnels
Cities and towns
Places of interest
Rivers
Roads
Maps of the journey

The book gives an account of features of interest and beauty to be seen from the carriage window. It is intended that the book be read in the train, and may be commenced at any point of the journey. A glance at the name of the station just passed, a reference to the Index, and what will be seen between there and the next station is described.

This book will be of great interest not only to passengers travelling on the steam-hauled heritage trains of today, but it will also appeal to railway enthusiasts, members of preserved railways, historians and tourists visiting the south coast of England. The book will be something that can be dipped into time and again. It is lavishly illustrated with a wealth of rare pictures showing the line in action during the great days of steam. The detailed text is enhanced by wonderful treasured artefacts from the bygone era of steam: timetables, tickets, signal box diagrams, train registers, loco rosters, nameplates etc.

This long-awaited book tells the remarkable story of Britain's last steam mainline from London. The aim has been to convey a special feeling for this nostalgic subject, as I was one who lived with and experienced the enormous pleasure that steam trains gave in everyday service during the 1950s and '60s. Regular visits to the locomotive sheds, Eastleigh Works and the stations along the line with my family instilled a deep love for the line. Over the years the sight and sound of each locomotive that passed through the New Forest at Beaulieu Road Station became very familiar and their footplate crews became a second family with a passing wave or whistle. It was almost like popping home to meet up with my railway family at the various engine sheds at Nine Elms, Basingstoke, Eastleigh, Bournemouth, Weymouth and Guildford. There was always a warm welcome on the footplate to reminisce with refreshment and a ride in the fireman's seat, while Dad took a hand on the shovel or on occasions the regulator. As my Aunt Doll was the owner of 'Dollies of Swaythling', the newsagents and tobacconists, railway customers from Eastleigh Shed and the Works would often leave messages for my father or myself about any exciting, interesting or unusual railway activities. On one occasion a Q Class steam locomotive hauling the Dorchester goods train slowed to a crawl, whistling furiously as I was walking across Matley Heath near Beaulieu Road Station in the New Forest; the driver tossed a handwritten message for my father, which was tied to a lump of coal saying: 'GWR Castle impounded at Eastleigh on its way to Portsmouth.' On another occasion I was hastily woken from my sleep one summer evening to help my parents and sister extinguish a fire in a dry gorse bush that had been started by the passing up mail train hauled by a Great Western Hall Class. My childhood memories of the Waterloo to Wessex line could fill a book in their own right, including the preservation of Merchant Navy Class 35028 *Clan Line* and raising the first £50 to purchase her, but that is for another day.

I dedicate this book to my sister, Ruth, who has encouraged me on an almost daily basis and reminded me of so many happy memories of our childhood days in the New Forest at Beaulieu Road station.

1

WATERLOO

The beginning of the journey from Waterloo was always exciting in steam days, with crack trains such as the *Bournemouth Belle*, *Atlantic Coast Express*, *Royal Wessex* and *Ocean Liner Express* boat trains departing daily. It is close to the south bank of the River Thames and a station on this site was first constructed in 1848 on raised arches over marshy ground. In 1899 the London & South Western Railway commenced rebuilding and expansion of the station, but this was not completed until 1922 owing to the First World War. Waterloo was the undeniable pride of place of the London & South Western Railway and after 1923 the Southern Railway, with twenty-one platforms and a concourse of 800ft. Day and night the station was a hive of furious activity with the morning and evening rush hours reaching a crescendo. In the dead of night and during the early hours in steam days Waterloo Station witnessed the departure of Royal Mail trains and newspaper trains to the south and west.

Passengers climb the steps and pass through the main pedestrian entrance called Victory Arch, which is a memorial to the staff that fell in both world wars. During the first few months of the Second World War, Waterloo Station became the scene of many painful departures for evacuees to the countryside as hoards of bewildered children escaped the Blitz. The station was a principal target for the German Luftwaffe and suffered damage during an air raid, temporarily stopping the train service. The section of line from Waterloo to Queen's Road was the most heavily attacked section of line in the country, being bombed and machine-gunned from the air no less than ninety-two times between September 1940 and May 1941.

Electric trains first appeared at Waterloo in 1915 and the system was expanded up to 1939. Eventually, with the electrification of the line to Southampton and Bournemouth, steam finally surrendered on 9 July 1967. In the final years of steam traction it was possible to witness clusters of railway enthusiasts congregating at the ends of the platforms at Waterloo festooned with cameras, tape recorders, cine equipment and their ever faithful *ABC* Ian Allan trainspotting books. As soon as a new locomotive came into sight they would quickly record the engine number, look it up in their *ABC* spotter's book and underline the number if it was previously unseen. This was a ritual repeated far and wide across post-war Britain and is now but a distant memory. Significantly, Waterloo was to become London's last main-line terminus with steam-hauled trains.

The station has also acted as a location set for many films including John Schlesinger's famous 1961 documentary *Terminus* and more recently *The Bourne Ultimatum*, starring Matt Damon. The station has also inspired artists with Helen McKie's poster commissions *Waterloo Station War* and *Waterloo Station Peace*, in which the artist has painted exactly the same scene with identical poses and portraits of figures, but with altered contrasting clothing and roles. The artist Terence Cuneo also recorded the scene on a huge canvas in 1967, complete with the inclusion of his signature mouse.

As the train winds out of Waterloo across the sharp curves, there is a spectacular view from the carriage window on the right-hand side of the Houses of Parliament, Big Ben and Westminster Abbey across the river. The tree-hedged Lambeth Palace, the home of the Archbishop of Canterbury, can be seen a little further on. When the train gathers speed, look out on the right for the long façade and glass dome of the Tate Gallery.

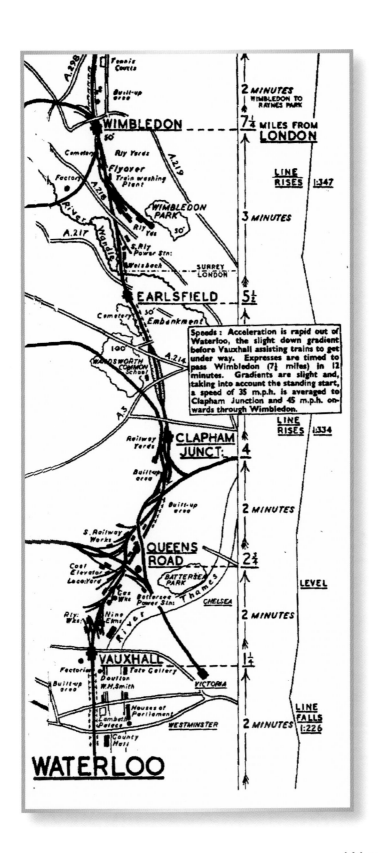

WIMBLEDON

A panoramic view of Waterloo taken from the Shell building in York Road in July 1965, showing an un-rebuilt Bulleid Pacific heading away from platform 10 with a train to Southampton, Bournemouth and Weymouth. In the next platform a Merchant Navy Pacific awaits release to work a light engine to Nine Elms, having arrived minutes earlier from Bournemouth. Meanwhile a BR Standard 4 80xxx Class tank waits in platform 12 and a Standard Class 5 in platform 13. An unidentified engine is lifting its safety valves with a white plume of steam in platform 7. (Britton Collection)

Guests arriving at platform 11 at Waterloo for the Mauretania Regent Refinery opening's special train to Southampton Docks were presented with red carnations for their buttonholes by smartly uniformed hostesses on 27 October 1964. (Valero Energy/Texaco)

A conversation piece at Waterloo in 1966, as the footplate crew of Merchant Navy Class No. 35007 *Aberdeen Commonwealth* chat with railway enthusiasts. (Britton Collection)

The preserved Drummond T9 No. 120 at Waterloo Station on the LCGB 'The Sussex Coast Limited Rail Tour' on 24 June. It was a scorching hot summer's day and 120 hauled the first leg of the tour from Waterloo to Horsham. (Britton Collection)

The time is approaching 12.30 p.m. as the preserved rebuilt Merchant Navy Class No. 35005 *Canadian Pacific* is at the head of the *Bournemouth Belle* Pullman car train. The down *Belle* will call at Southampton Central at 1.58 p.m., Bournemouth Central at 2.40 p.m. and arrive at Bournemouth West at 2.52 p.m. (Britton Collection)

Drummond M7 tank No. 30039 and an unidentified former GWR Pannier tank are busy at Waterloo Station, shunting empty carriage stock to and from Clapham sidings. (Britton Collection)

The smiling face of the fireman peers out from the cab of rebuilt Merchant Navy Class No. 35023 *Holland Africa Line* at Waterloo Station. The fireman has built up his fire well for the journey ahead to Southampton and Bournemouth, and the safety valves are lifting, indicating that the boiler pressure is at 250lb/sq.in. (John Cox)

2

VAUXHALL TO CLAPHAM JUNCTION

As the train accelerates through Vauxhall, just yards from the banks of the River Thames there are wonderful views across the capital. When steam traction ruled, railway enthusiasts' heads would be turning to the left at this point, to catch a glimpse of Nine Elms locomotive shed. Nine Elms (or 70A as it was coded by British Railways) was strategically positioned to serve Waterloo Station. Movements in and out of the shed were controlled by the Loco Junction signal box, which was straddled over the main line on supporting cast iron girders. The Elms supplied locomotives for the Waterloo–Southampton–Bournemouth and Waterloo–Salisbury–Exeter lines, in addition to local duties with carriage shunting and the Kennington local (known as the 'Kenny Belle').

The facilities at Nine Elms were dominated by a turntable from which all the access lines radiated. These roads led to two covered sheds. The Old Shed was a fifteen-road brick-built dead-end shed with a corrugated asbestos roof. This half-roofed building had suffered bomb damage during the Second World War and was patched up. During the final years of steam it was gradually demolished and was an open-air storage yard. Next door to this was the New Shed, which was a ten-road covered brick-built shed, remaining in use until closure. Perhaps the most impressive feature at the Elms was the massive 400-ton concrete-built coaling hopper. The exit rails to the coaling hopper had subsided a few inches over the years, which created a slight upward gradient. This caused the Bulleid Pacifics to amusingly 'loose their feet', especially if the rail surface was greasy!

In 1960, Nine Elms Shed had a very impressive allocation of over 100 locomotives, including a fine array of ex-South Eastern Region Schools Class, L1, E1 and H Class engines. The Schools Class were put to work on the Lymington trains, and I regularly saw them at Beaulieu Road Station or coming off at Brockenhurst due to Lymington branch weight restrictions. The L1 and E1 engines appeared to linger in the Old Shed with infrequent use. During the final few years the locomotive allocation began to dwindle and by 1967 there were a mere twenty-four on the books. In 1964, the Merchant Navy Class Pacifics were reallocated to Weymouth Shed owing to poor maintenance facilities, but they reappeared for the final few months of their lives and were restored to the Nine Elms allocation.

Nine Elms provided locomotives for 'carriage bopping' duties between Waterloo and Clapham Junction sidings. The tank engines on these duties would haul the empty carriage stock into the platforms at Waterloo and then assist the departing train engine with a gentle push out. From

1959 onwards, ten Western Region 57xx Pannier tanks were rostered to Nine Elms for these duties to replace the regular but ageing M7 tanks. They in turn were replaced by BR Standard 4MT 80xxx, 3MT 82xxx and Ivatt 2MT tanks. These tank engines proved to be roomy for footplate crews and efficient. Nine Elms footplate crews did not appreciate the Western Panniers, which they regarded as cramped and uncomfortable on the footplate. Further complaints were voiced about the Panniers 'hunting' from side to side and poor steaming. From their first appearance at the Elms in January 1959, problems were encountered with the Western system of 21in vacuum brakes and, consequently, when a Southern engine took over for a main-line run, the carriage brakes would drag. Additionally, Nine Elms firemen complained that the Panniers constantly required topping up with water to replenish their tanks. On the plus side, the Panniers were found to be strong and could easily handle Waterloo–Clapham Yard stock workings. When they were eventually replaced in July 1963 there were few tears shed by the Elms crews.

Perhaps the most popular class of engines allocated to Nine Elms from August 1955 were the BR Standard Class 5s Nos 73110–119. Following a suggestion from Mr H.F. Wood of the Nine Elms stalwart of the white-collar staff, the names of withdrawn Urie King Arthur 4-6-0s were adopted by the Southern Standard 5s in May 1958. The nameplates were similar to those on the original King Arthur Class in that they were straight with tapered ends, but they did not carry the legend 'King Arthur Class' under the name. Theses nameplates were fitted to the engines as they passed through Eastleigh Works without any formal ceremony and mounted on the valance of the footplate with the centre of the nameplate positioned level with the centre line of the dome. They soon gained the nickname, 'the Standard Arthurs'. From May 1959, the Derby-built Standard Five sisters 73080–89 originally allocated to Stewarts Lane Shed were transferred to the Elms.

What is not commonly known is that there were visual detail differences between the Doncaster- and Derby-built Class 5s allocated to Nine Elms. The Derby-built Class Fives had their whistle placed behind the chimney, where the Doncaster Standard 5s had their whistle mounted on the top of the firebox casing. The numbers painted on the cabs of the Doncaster 5s were slightly larger in appearance with the cab front windows hinged to allow for better window cleaning. When first allocated to Nine Elms, the Standard 5s with their distinctive large 5,625-gallon water capacity BR1F type tenders with 7 tons of coal had teething problems. Nine Elms footplate crews initially complained that their new Standard 5s were poor steamers. Branksome Shed's Peter Smith often relates that he was one of those who put the Nine Elms crews on the path to success for handling Standard 5s. Peter, who is nowadays the volunteer Swanage Railway Locomotive Inspector, reminisces that he was invited up on to 73111 at Branksome by a Nine Elms fireman: 'How do you S & D blokes get on wiv these Standard 5s mate? Us lot at the Elms can't make 'em steam properly.' Peter soon put the Nine Elms fireman right by selecting a few choice lumps of coal from the tender and placing them on the fire by hand to build up a good depth of fire under the fire hole door and tapered it down to the front end. Additionally, the distinguished Branksome-based Somerset & Dorset fireman Smith unblocked the back damper with ash and clinker in order to provide the Standard 5 with a better air flow. The result was a free-steaming engine. The secret of success on how to fire a Standard 5 soon spread around Nine Elms and the Standard 5s proved to be Nine Elms' favourite engines. They had self-cleaning smoke boxes and rocking drop grates, which aided the fireman considerably. The Nine

Elms 5s would on occasions be called upon to deputise for Bulleid Merchant Navy Class and with Nine Elms crews at the controls would rise to the occasion and challenge of heavy express trains.

In the final years there was a variety of visiting locomotives from other regions to haul enthusiast specials. Many of these special trains used engines prepared at Nine Elms, for action on the Bournemouth–Weymouth line. For some reason many LNER locomotives featured included the K4 *The Great Marquess*, A4s *Mallard*, *Kingfisher* and *Sir Nigel Gresley*, A2 *Blue Peter* and A3 *Flying Scotsman*. Driver Bert Hooker related to my father that the secret of success with the visiting North Eastern engines was to ensure that they were supplied with good-quality hard Yorkshire coal. On the occasion of the visit of the A4 *Mallard* in 1963, Bert recalled that not only did she arrive from King's Cross Top Shed in immaculate condition, but also with a wagon full of Yorkshire coal!

The visiting ex-LNER engines were a credit to the hard work of those who prepared them at Nine Elms, with two exceptions: the A2 Class 60532 *Blue Peter* and V2 60919. *Blue Peter* had been sent down to London from Scotland to work the LCGB 'A2 Commemorative Rail Tour' on 14 August 1966. She arrived at Nine Elms in very poor condition with her centre cylinder drain cocks stuck open. Despite the thorough and meticulous preparation, plus top-notch driving from the Nine Elms driver Clive Groome, the A2 Pacific did not perform well. The ongoing centre drain cock problem combined with the tender full of Nine Elms 'bug dust' coal resulted in poor steaming on her run down to Exeter. This in turn led to a stop on Honiton Bank for a blow up with running repairs and attention at Exmouth Junction Shed, resulting in a delay of three hours for passengers on the LCGB special. The special train eventually returned from Westbury to Waterloo behind a Britannia 70004 *William Shakespeare*.

The second LNER sinner to visit Nine Elms was the V2 60919 from Dundee in Scotland. She took five days to work south ready for the LCGB 'Green Arrow Rail Tour' of 3 July 1966. The V2 arrived at the Elms in a very run-down condition with a broken spring and was declared a failure and replaced by West Country Class 34002 *Salisbury*. Fitters at Nine Elms set to work and made a valiant effort to repair the V2 in order that she could haul at least part of the route of the special train. The 60919 set off light engine to Eastleigh ready to resume her special duties, but upon arrival at Eastleigh it was discovered that the right-hand water supply to the injector would not shut off. This fault was repaired by fitter Bob Joy at Eastleigh, but by this time Control declared that it had lost its path. The Scottish visitor was then sent back up to Nine Elms, but at Micheldever suffered an overheated inside small end only to be stopped at Basingstoke.

Another welcome visiting class of engine in latter years was the ex-LMS Black Fives, which were regularly serviced when 'borrowed' by Bournemouth Shed for the weekend. Nine Elms crews openly said they were a treat to work on and could gallop away! Amusingly, although the Southern Railway had been nationalised into British Railways in 1947, some older drivers right up to the end referred to the Maunsell and Bulleid classes as 'Company' engines and other types as 'foreigners'.

It was a Nine Elms crew who had the honour of crewing 34051 *Winston Churchill* to haul the Winston Churchill funeral train from Waterloo to Handborough in Oxfordshire. On 30 January 1965, Nine Elms was given the special duty of covering the funeral train of the Second World War leader Sir Winston Churchill. For this special occasion, the un-rebuilt Bulleid Light Pacific 34051 *Winston Churchill* was prepared to pristine condition with sister engine 34064 *Fighter Command* as standby engine. Driver Alf Hurley and fireman Jim Lester had the great honour of crewing 34051. All along the line, crowds stood and watched the funeral train in silent respect, including all of my family. As 34051 passed it was a very emotional and solemn occasion as both of my parents had served their country during the Second World War.

At Nine Elms the practice was that each driver was teamed up with a regular fireman. This tradition did not extend to the lower links, which were made up of younger, less experienced drivers and those who were approaching retirement. On occasion firemen were 'borrowed' from Eastleigh, Fratton and Salisbury. There were supposed to be up to twenty-six cleaners at the Elms, but in the last few years of steam they did not exist. The shed had 200 registered drivers and firemen, plus a whole host of fitters, tool men, office staff, turntable operators, ash cleaners, fire lighters, coalmen, store men and a head code man for maintaining the white loco discs. They were all great characters and a very welcoming bunch of men. In the last few months of steam, many of the footplate crews would thrash their engines by 'going for the ton'.

Trains not allocated to Nine Elms arriving at Waterloo from the Bournemouth and Salisbury lines required turning, watering and servicing. Engines working up to the capital did not always require coaling however. Almost up to the final days, Nine Elms was an extremely busy shed packed full of action.

When steam disappeared in July 1967, Nine Elms Shed was swept away and the site is now the new Covent Garden wholesale vegetable and fruit market.

Approaching Queen's Road Station, where the line from Victoria connects, passengers would look out for the iconic landmark chimneys of the now decommissioned Battersea Power Station. The power station became a celebrity location, with films such as The Beatles' *Help!* being filmed there in the 1960s and more recently a cameo appearance in Take That's *The Flood.* Since closure, it has remained largely unused.

As the journey continues out of London, the train passes Clapham Junction, where up to 2,500 trains per day pass, 100 of them an hour during the rush hour. In steam days former Great Western Pannier tanks, Drummond M7, Ivatt *Mickey Mouse* and BR tanks rushed around the sidings marshalling heavy train sets of carriages 'twixt Clapham and Waterloo. To railway enthusiasts it was paradise, a vast expanse of tracks, points, crossovers, signal gantries, platforms and bridges, where as many as half a dozen steam engines at a time could be seen shunting or roaring through – a triumph in signal control and organisation.

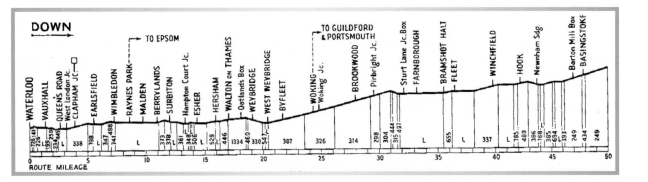

Framed by the Vauxhall Station canopy and with a backdrop of Big Ben and the Houses of Parliament, rebuilt Merchant Navy No. 35028 *Clan Line* charges through Vauxhall Station on 28 February 1967 with a fast bound for Southampton, Bournemouth and Weymouth. (Britton Collection)

Green Southern Region station signs for Vauxhall almost obliterate the identification of rebuilt Merchant Navy No. 35013 *Blue Funnel*. Originally this engine was named *Blue Funnel Line*, but new name plates were fitted in July 1945 with the words, *Blue Funnel Certum Pete Fineum*. The Latin phrase translates as 'make a good job of it'. No. 35013 was certainly making a good job of hauling the down *Royal Wessex* train in July 1966. (Britton Collection)

Ivatt tank No. 41298 skips away from Clapham Junction to Waterloo with an empty carriage stock working on 13 June 1967. (Britton Collection)

The last Clapham Junction–Kensington Olympia *Kennington Belle*, hauled by BR Standard 3 tank No. 82019 on 7 July 1967. The four-coach green liveried set included the experimental glass-fibre-bodied vehicle No. S1000. (Britton Collection)

By 1967 the scene had changed at Nine Elms to one of neglect, with choking weeds between the neglected rusting rails that were home to the predominating BR Standards and Bulleid Pacifics. (Britton Collection)

'Quiet Please. Avoid annoyance to residents and take care to avoid smoke and steam', proclaimed the sign on the 3 July 1967. 'My dear boy, who do they think they are kidding?' actor and railway enthusiast Kenneth More would comment each time he visited Nine Elms Shed. The little Ivatt tank was a real workhorse and was predominantly occupied on Clapham sidings–Waterloo carriage workings. Ivatt 41298 is now preserved at Haven Street on the Isle of Wight Steam Railway, thanks to the Ivatt Trust. (Britton Collection)

BR Standard 4 75075 with BR Standard 4 tank 80145 behind her inside the depths of Nine Elms New Shed on 12 March 1967. The smell within the dark, smoky depths of Nine Elms Shed was of steam, hot oil and coal – something to savour and remember. (Britton Collection)

Record-breaking LNER A4 60022 *Mallard* is polished to perfection outside Nine Elms Shed ready for driver Bert Hooker and fireman Bob Payne on Sunday 23 February 1963. She arrived complete with a wagon of Yorkshire coal! Bert often recalled that the A4 racehorse achieved 93mph through Andover whilst working an enthusiast special. (Britton Collection)

3

CLAPHAM JUNCTION TO SURBITON

Heading away from Clapham Junction the journey continues down the busy main line, passing Wandsworth Common and through Earlsfield. The name Earlsfield originates from the large Victorian residence formerly on the site of the station. When the Davis family sold the land to the railway company it was on condition that the new station would be called Earlsfield.

The railway now passes over the River Wandle, which derives its name from the Old English word, *Wendlesworth*, meaning Wendle's Settlement. Today much of the river is accessible by the Wandle Trail.

From 5 July 1936 the reinforced concrete railway flyover approaching Wimbledon allowed a more frequent electric train service to the suburbs. Adjacent to the line was the former carriage maintenance depot and washing plant – now a modern, efficient, electric train care facility. The present centre cannot be seen from the carriage window, but the original championship ground is passed close to the line just past the station. The line here first opened on 21 May 1838 and the original station was to the south of the current station on the opposite side of Wimbledon Bridge. The current station building was constructed by the Southern Railway and is made from Portland Stone in an art deco design.

Steam-hauled trains would open up beyond Wimbledon towards Raynes Park. This is the junction for the line to Epsom. Up until 1970 it was possible to catch a glimpse of an array of colour from the left-hand side of the train during the spring and summer at the James Carter & Co. seed-testing premises. For the brave person with his head out of the carriage window it was even possible to smell the sweet perfumes of ornamental flowers, if the train had cause to stop for a signal check or slow for a permanent way slack. On the opposite side of the train is the Southern Railway Sports Ground. It was here that the Nine Elms Railway football team used to play all their home games. During the summer months the grounds became a haven for cricket.

Before entering New Malden, the railway passes over Beverley Brook, a small tributary to the River Thames, which runs through Beverley Park. On the right-hand side of the train is the 120-acre mature parkland golf course founded in 1893. The land that now forms this lush course was originally part of the Coombe Manor Estate, which had been acquired from Queen Elizabeth I in 1579. It sweeps over Hogsmill river and past Berrylands, an historic settlement that can trace its origins back to Anglo-Saxon times. The next section of line is through a long cutting to Surbiton, where steam trains frequently ignited the lineside vegetation.

The preserved LNER K4 Class No. 3442 *The Great Marquess,* which has been prepared at Nine Elms Shed, passes Wandsworth Common with empty carriage stock for an enthusiast special on 12 March 1967. (Britton Collection)

Rebuilt Merchant Navy Class No. 35014 *Netherland Line* speeds along the embankment past Russell Cabinets storage yard, opposite Summerley Street, just west of Earlsfield on 12 March 1967. (Britton Collection)

What could be more English than a cricket match on Wimbledon Common and the sight and sound of a passing steam train? Photographer Chris Gammell has captured this scene of yesteryear to perfection as rebuilt Bulleid Pacific No. 34090 *Sir Eustace Missenden* passes on the 6.43 p.m. Waterloo–Southampton Docks boat train on 14 June 1967. (C.J. Gammell/Britton Collection)

London South Western Railway opened Durnsford Road Power Station, Wimbledon, in 1915 to supply electricity as part of the electrification plan. Positioned on the north side of the line, it closed in the mid-1960s, with the last chimney being demolished in February 1965. The electric depot seen on the left of the picture has been modernised as a train care depot by South West Trains. Here the down *Atlantic Coast Express*, hauled by rebuilt Merchant Navy Class No. 35030 *Elder Dempster Lines,* accelerates past on 30 August 1958. (Martin Robinson Collection)

Un-rebuilt Battle of Britain Bulleid 4-6-2 Pacific No. 34080 *74 Squadron* approaches Raynes Park with the 1.00 p.m. Waterloo–Plymouth on 2 August 1964. (Britton Collection)

92220 *Evening Star* storms through Surbiton on the Ian Allan Eastleigh Works Rail Tour on 3 April 1964. (John Cox)

4

SURBITON TO WOKING

The main line to the south-west was originally intended to run through Kingston, but the Kingston Corporation objected, fearing an impact on their coaching trade, so the course of the railway passed about 1½ miles south of the town, opening in 1838. Seven years later the station was resited from King Charles Road to a mile west to Surbiton. The short branch line to Hampton Court opened on 1 February 1849 with the line to Effingham Junction and Guildford opening on 2 February 1885 (known as the 'New Guildford Line'). This made Surbiton an important junction connecting station.

The London & South Western Railway had some difficulty in deciding on a name for the station until 1867 when the sign Surbiton appeared on the platforms. Prior to this the station name boards and tickets referred to the station as Kingston Junction, from 1852, changing to Surbiton and Kingston in 1863.

The present Surbiton Station was rebuilt in 1937 by the Southern Railway, with two island platforms and attractive canopies. The station was at one time equipped with a moderately sized goods yard, which was situated on the eastern 'down' side of the station and there were two additional sidings on the western 'up' side with a short loading platform. Between 1960 and 1964 British Railways Southern Region ran a car carrier service from Surbiton to Okehampton, shadowing the route of the *Atlantic Coast Express*.

Beyond Surbiton the scenery changes and yellow flowering gorse can be seen from the carriage window covering the Common to Esher. During the summer months it is home to many butterflies and moths. The station at Esher is recognisable by its distinctive characteristic wooden footbridge. Prior to electrification of the Bournemouth line in 1967, the station was dominated by a tall signal gantry with the platforms offering a Southern Railway atmosphere with concrete lamp standards carrying characteristic hexagonal lampshades. Leaving the station on the left-hand side of the train is the famous Sandown Racecourse. Opened in 1875, the course was the favourite of the Queen Mother and is now a popular venue for many pop concerts. The racecourse owes its success to the railway, as the masses travelled down on trains from the capital.

Our train now speeds over the ancient River Mole, which can trace its origins back to the Ice Age, the mid-Pleistocene period just over half a million years ago. Domesday Book lists twenty water mills on the River Mole, one of which can be glimpsed from the 'down' passing train on the right-hand side, before entering Hersham. The station at Hersham is located about a mile north of the village, which makes returning home from a night out in the capital a bit of a trek – especially if it is raining!

The next station on the line is Walton on Thames Station, which opened as 'Walton for Hersham'. Between Walton and Weybridge a long cutting obscures the view from the train. Before entering Weybridge, the line to Chertsey diverges off on the right and it crosses over the River Wey. On the left-hand side are the remnants of Brooklands race track, which opened in 1907 and held its last race in 1939. It could host up to 287,000 spectators in its heyday. Located just 19 miles from Waterloo, Weybridge Station is in a cavernous and dramatic setting deep in a cutting. The main station buildings are at street level on the up side of the station, linked to the platforms by stairs and a footbridge.

The line from Waterloo has up to now been on the level, but approaching West Byfleet, the final station before Woking, the line begins a long climb of some 10½ miles at 1 in 314 to 1 in 387 to the summit at Brookwood.

Rebuilt Bulleid West Country Class No. 34037 approaching Esher, hauling the 6.20 p.m. Waterloo–Southampton Docks train, on 8 July 1967. This was the locomotive's final revenue-earning working. Note her nameplates, attached for the occasion. The following day was the final day of steam on the Southern. (Britton Collection)

The late afternoon sunshine on 18 March 1967 shines down on rebuilt West Country Class No. 34047 *Callington* as it crosses Weybridge Viaduct with the 4.15 p.m. Feltham–Eastleigh freight. It was not unusual to see steam Bulleid Pacifics hauling freight trains in those final months of steam traction on the Southern. (C.J. Gammell/Britton Collection)

The down *Atlantic Coast Express* whisks through Woking in August 1964, hauled by an unidentified rebuilt Bulleid Merchant Navy Pacific. (Britton Collection)

A brief stop at Woking allows the fireman on rebuilt West Country Class No. 34044 *Woolacombe* to top up the 4,500-gallon tender with water, in this October 1966 view. (Britton Collection)

British Railways Southern Region unusually permitted the Army's Longmoor Military Railway 2-10-0 No. 600 *Gordon* to enter Woking to haul an enthusiast special on 30 April 1966. Today this magnificent blue-liveried engine is preserved at the Severn Valley Railway in Worcestershire. (Britton Collection)

Rebuilt Bulleid Pacific No. 34060 *25 Squadron* clatters away from Woking with a Bournemouth semi-fast train on 3 June 1967. (Britton Collection)

No. 36A

BRITISH RAILWAYS

19th SEPTEMBER 1955
AND UNTIL FURTHER NOTICE

TRAIN SERVICE
AND FARES

BETWEEN

LONDON
(WATERLOO)

SURBITON, WOKING

AND

BROOKWOOD
(for the London Necropolis)

ALDERSHOT, FARNBOROUGH

WATERLOO STATION,
LONDON, S.E.1.

T.W. 5146/ A11 11855
B.R. 35034/19

Printed by
Stringer, Briggs, Stockley & Co.,
Kingston

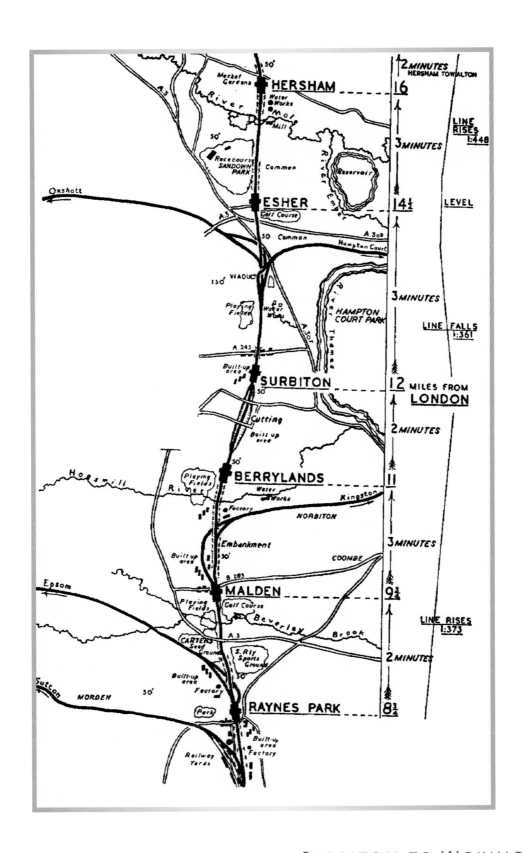

5

WOKING TO BROOKWOOD

Woking was the first major stopping point out of Waterloo for steam-hauled services up to July 1967. Here the main line divides beyond the once busy railway yards, left to Guildford, Portsmouth and Southsea, right to Farnborough, Basingstoke and the south-west. On the left-hand side is the first mosque to be built in Britain in 1899, the Shah Jahan Mosque.

Woking is also famed to all railway workers for the Woking Southern Railwaymen's Home for Children and Old People. Initially it accepted children over the age of 6 who had lost their railwaymen fathers. Many were not orphans, however, as financial concerns forced mothers from railway families to choose an orphanage upbringing for their children. The orphanage was primarily funded through voluntary contributions, the bulk of which originated from employees of the Southern Railway and later British Railway Southern Region. It also appealed to the public to donate at flag days and on the platforms of railway stations, where dogs with collecting boxes publicised the work of the Home, which could accommodate 150 children. In the 1960s part of the Woking Homes began to cater for retired railway personnel and their spouses. In steam days many engine drivers would offer enthusiasts and photographers unofficial footplate rides in return for a donation to the Woking Homes. Driver Eddie Prangnell, on his Adams O2 tank engine, based at Ryde St John's Road Shed on the Isle of Wight, raised hundreds of pounds for the Homes each summer in this way!

The sighting of a signal outside the windows of the signal box at Woking made smoky stopping steam trains very unpopular. Complaints about overenthusiastic firemen from the signalmen were often met with lumps of coal thrown over as compensation for use in the signal-box stove. The considerable freight yards at Woking to the west of the station became a Mecca for railway enthusiasts in the last few years of steam, as engineering trains with rail and ballast assembled to assist with the electrification of the line to Bournemouth. Veteran Maunsell moguls and Bulleid Q1 Class from Guildford Shed were provided to haul these heavy freight trains and thus contribute to their own ultimate doom.

The next station is Brookwood, which is famous for its cemetery. At one time funeral trains ran down from Waterloo into one of two special platforms within the cemetery. The famous Scottish-bred London South Western Railway locomotive engineer Dugald Drummond is buried in the cemetery. It was said by many Nine Elms and Eastleigh Shed drivers of Drummond-designed locomotives that, as they roared through Brookwood thrashing their engines, a ghostly figure would appear on the platforms at Brookwood shaking his fist. Hence it became an unofficial tradition when passing through Brookwood that all drivers of Drummond-designed engines would either whistle in salute or dip their greaseproof caps. According to the late driver Bert Hooker, this tradition was maintained to the end, when the Drummond T9 locomotive No. 120 passed through for the final time with an enthusiast special.

The race is on! Leaving Woking on 27 February 1967, Bournemouth driver Stan Symes (complete with his American-style engineman's cap) fully opens the regulator on rebuilt West Country No. 34093 *Saunton* to rapidly accelerate to over 70mph. Stan was always up for a challenge and was determined to pass the electric multiple unit, thrashing 34021 to give her best. Within minutes the smiling Bournemouth driver was cheekily lifting his cap and blowing the engine's whistle in salute to his colleague on the electric train as *Saunton* confidently accelerated past. (Britton Collection)

BR Standard 5 No. 73155 glides through Brookwood on the fast-line centre rails. The Standard 5s were very popular engines on the Southern, and this particular Guildford-based engine was artist David Shepherd's favourite. (Alan Sainty Collection)

The time is just after 10.30 a.m. on July 1967 at Brookwood. This is a very sad occasion for steam on the Southern as rebuilt Merchant Navy Class No. 35008 Orient Line hauls BR's 'Farewell to Southern Steam' special. (Britton Collection)

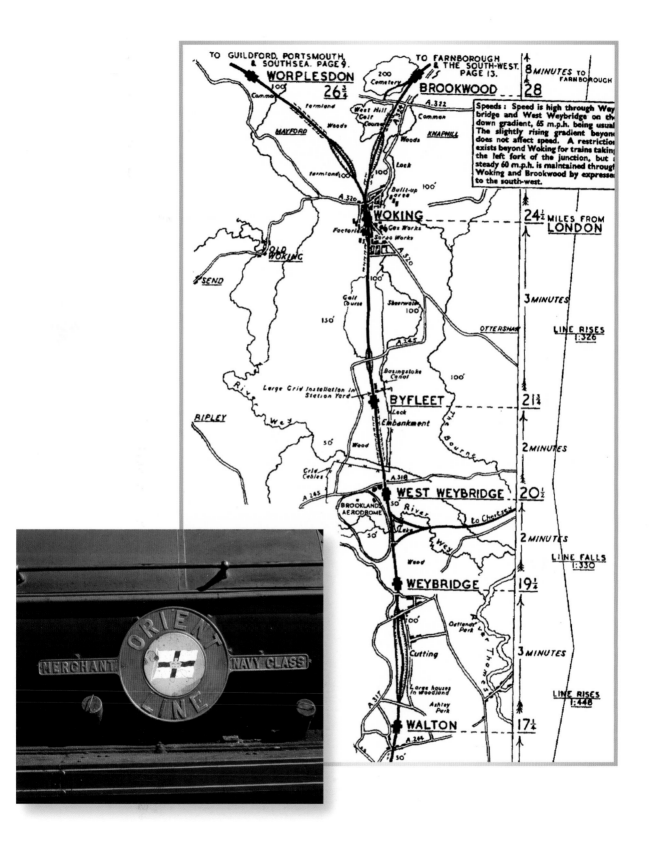

TO GUILDFORD, PORTSMOUTH
& SOUTHSEA. PAGE 9.

TO FARNBOROUGH
& THE SOUTH-WEST.
PAGE 13.

8 MINUTES TO FARNBOROUGH

WORPLESDON 26¾

200 Cemetery

BROOKWOOD 28

A.322

Common

West Hill Golf Course

MAYFORD

Woods

Woods

KNAPHILL

Common

farmland

Lock

A.320

farmland 100'

Built-up area

100'

Speeds : Speed is high through Weybridge and West Weybridge on the
down gradient, 65 m.p.h. being usual.
The slightly rising gradient beyond
does not affect speed. A restriction
exists beyond Woking for trains taking
the left fork of the junction, but a
steady 60 m.p.h. is maintained through
Woking and Brookwood by expresses
to the south-west.

WOKING

Factories Gas Works

Sewage Works

A.320

24½ MILES FROM
LONDON

OLD WOKING

SEND

100'

Golf Course

Sheerwater 100'

150'

A.245

OTTERSHAW

3 MINUTES

LINE RISES
1:326

River Wey

RIPLEY

Basingstoke Canal

Large Grid Installation in
Station Yard

100'

BYFLEET 21¼

Lock

Embankment

Bourne

50'

Wood

Grid Cables

2 MINUTES

A.245

A.318

50'

WEST WEYBRIDGE 20½

BROOKLANDS
AERODROME

50'

River

to Chertsey

Wey

Lake

50'

River Thames

Wood

2 MINUTES

LINE FALLS
1:330

WEYBRIDGE 19½

Oatlands Park

100'

Cutting

3 MINUTES

A.317

Large houses
in Woodland

Ashley Park

LINE RISES
1:448

WALTON 17¼

A.244

50'

6

BROOKWOOD TO WINCHFIELD

Heading down the main line from Brookwood the train passes Bisley Camp and Army ranges on the right-hand side and Pirbright Common on the left. This military training area was known to generations of 'squaddies' with their .303 rifles and Bren guns under the supervision of screaming sergeant majors! At Pirbright Junction the line to Alton diverges with another flyover.

Approaching Farnborough the railway runs parallel to the old Basingstoke Canal, which was built in 1794 to connect Basingstoke with the River Thames at Weybridge via the Wey Navigation. The canal was never a commercial success and from 1950, with lack of maintenance, the canal was derelict and overgrown. After years of neglect, however, restoration commenced as far as Greywell Tunnel in 1977 and was completed on 10 May 1991. Unfortunately, insufficient water supplies, problems with funding and conservation issues have prevented the full restoration of the Basingstoke Canal. The railway passes under the aqueduct just prior to the junction for the line to Frimley and Reading.

Farnborough Station was opened in 1838 and would later become the stop where thousands of airmen belonging to the Royal Air Force Photographic Squadron alighted. Since the Second World War the airfield has been the venue of the Farnborough Air Show and when this is on, passengers of passing trains have been treated to fly pasts and displays ranging from the Battle of Britain flight to the latest supersonic aircraft. It is said that Queen Victoria temporarily used Farnborough Station to get to Windsor Castle, though the main station she used was Slough until Windsor had its own station.

At Fleet the countryside becomes beautifully wooded. The station here was originally opened as Fleet Pond, but when the station was remodelled to four tracks it became Fleet on 1 July 1869. In 1906 the station expanded as the local population grew. After the fall of France in 1940, an up train from Bournemouth to Waterloo, hauled by a King Arthur Class travelling at 75mph travelling through Fleet, was strafed by a German Junkers 88 aircraft. The aircraft's machine-gun bullets rained down along the side of the engine as the gunner was aiming for the boiler, but somehow the driver with the engine's regulator fully open outran the menacing twin-engine aircraft.

Before entering the next station on the line at Winchfield, we pass over the River Hart. Winchfield serves the village of the same name and Hartley Wintney and other surrounding villages in rural Hampshire. The station was opened as Shapley Heath on 24 September 1838 as a temporary terminus, but renamed Winchfield in October 1840. The wide gap between the two platforms and their tracks dates back to the time when there was an island platform. When the station expanded and rebuilt with canopies, this island platform was removed and the centre tracks were realigned for faster running.

Leaving Winchfield across the ancient Shapley Heath, the view from the carriage window is obscured by a deep cutting. As the view clears the line travels along a high embankment across the River Whitewater, which rises at springs near Bidden Grange Farm between Upton Grey and Greywell. This beautiful chalk stream is rich with wildlife and contains a variety of fine fish for the angler, including brown trout, dace, barbell, perch, pike, roach and chub.

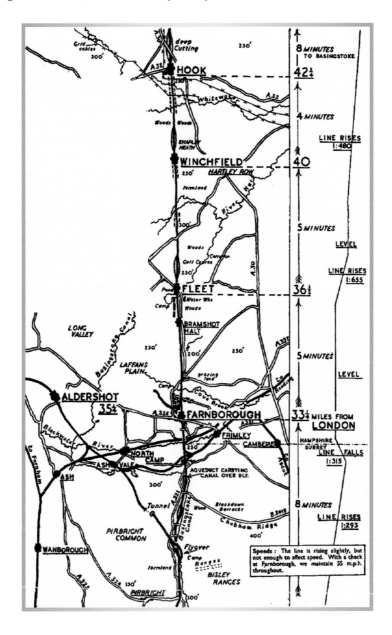

Passing at speed: A mile south of Farnborough, rebuilt Merchant Navy Class No. 35029 *Ellerman Lines* is seen approaching in the opposite direction with an express service to Bournemouth on board rebuilt West Country Class No. 34004 *Yeovil*, on 4 June 1966. (Britton Collection)

Bulleid Light Pacific No. 34073 *249 Squadron* is pictured hauling the down *Bournemouth Belle* in 1963 near Fleet, heading under an impressive lower quadrant LSWR pneumatic signal gantry. (Britton Collection)

BR Standard Class 5 4-6-0 No. 73087 *Linette* pauses in Arctic conditions at Fleet Station with a stopping train. (Alan Sainty Collection)

King Arthur Class 4-6-0 No. 30796 *Sir Dodinas le Savage* heads away from Fleet Station on 19 August 1961. (Alan Sainty Collection)

Lord Nelson Class 4-6-0 No. 30856 *Lord St Vincent* is a fine sight as she passes through Winchfield Station on 8 August 1959. (Britton Collection)

Rebuilt Bulleid Light Pacific
No. 34082 *615 Squadron*
strides through Winchfield
Cutting with a down semi-
fast train to Bournemouth
on 15 May 1965. (Britton
Collection)

Bulleid West Country Class
No. 34015 *Exmouth*, in
original condition, hauling
the 5.00 p.m. from Waterloo
to Exeter at speed through
the tree-lined Winchfield
Cutting, pictured from the
high vantage point of Old
Potbridge Road Bridge on
20 June 1964. (Britton
Collection)

No. 76026 is seen
approaching Winchfield
Station from the west on
8 August 1959, with the
tall Old Potbridge Road
Bridge visible in the distance.
(Britton Collection)

7

WINCHFIELD TO BASINGSTOKE

Hook is the next railway station, opening in 1883 after a campaign by local landowners. The station was originally constructed with two platforms and two lines, but was rebuilt to four platforms in 1902. In the early 1960s British Railways removed the island platform to facilitate high-speed running. Tragedy hit the station in 1940 when six bomb disposal officers were killed and a sergeant injured attempting to defuse an unexploded German bomb. The local residents have placed a memorial plaque to commemorate them in the station.

Heading west from Hook the railway enters another deep cutting before heading along an embankment crossing the River Lyde. A second river, the River Loddon, is crossed near Basing Mill on a brick-built railway viaduct with four arches. Historically the River Loddon has been important for milling and the channel has been modified with the creation of mill ponds and sluices. Old Basing Mill was a corn mill and is now called Barton's Mill.

Basingstoke, 47¾ miles from London, was without doubt one of the best places to watch steam in action on the Southern. The station was a busy junction for the Southampton–Bournemouth–Weymouth and Salisbury–Exeter main line from Waterloo. Additionally there was the Western Region connection to Reading. Standing on the platform for an hour was an exciting prospect as it was possible to view passing expresses race through, see semi-fast stopping trains, inter-regional trains and freights. Who can forget the memory of prestige trains like the Pullman *Bournemouth Belle*, *Royal Wessex*, *Atlantic Coast Express* and Southampton boat expresses roaring through with their whistles screaming? When one had enough it was possible to wander around the shed located opposite on the down side of the station.

The London & Southampton Railway opened the first line into Basingstoke on 10 June 1839, with the section to Winchester and Southampton opening on 11 May 1840. The 13½-mile Great Western line to Reading was opened on 1 November 1848 as a broad-gauge line. This was converted to dual gauge operation with the first standard gauge service arriving at Basingstoke from Reading on 22 December 1856. The LSWR advanced the line westwards to Andover, opening on 3 July 1854 and Salisbury three years later in May 1857. A curious branch to Alton was opened in 1901, which was to gain fame as the location for the Gainsborough Film Productions, *The Wrecker* and *Oh Mr*

Porter. This line was never profitable and closed in 1932. During the First World War, a branch line was built to Park Prewitt Hospital.

To service all this traffic, the LSWR opened a small locomotive shed on the south side of the line, to the west of the station. This was closed in 1909 when restructuring of the station took place. A new shed was built on the north side of the line, west of the station. The Great Western opened a two-road timber-and-brick-built locomotive shed in 1905, positioned at the London end of the station on the north side. It was a sub-shed of Reading and when it closed in November 1950, the allocation of engines transferred to the Southern Shed. This slated-roof-and-glazed-gable-end three-road shed was equipped with a canopied coal stage and a 70ft turntable, which replaced the earlier 55ft turntable during the Second World War in 1943. It was coded by British Railways as 70D. Until 20 September 1963, when the shed was downgraded to a signing on point/stabling point, Basingstoke was notable in that it always had an engine in steam as cover for engine failure, similar to Grantham on the Eastern Region. After downgrading in 1963, Basingstoke came under the control of 71A Eastleigh, which in turn changed its shed code identification to 70D. Nevertheless, the shed and yard always seemed to have a locomotive presence right up to the end of steam in July 1967.

In addition to providing twenty-four-hour cover for engine failures, the shed used to provide engines to work stopping services to Salisbury and Waterloo, rush-hour semi-fasts to London, freight trip workings and shunters for the local yards. Adams G6 0-6-0 tanks, known to Basingstoke drivers as a Sally, were provided for shunting duties until July 1961, when a 350hp diesel replaced the last of them. A reliable Drummond Black Motor 700 Class was the usual motive power for local freight work up until Christmas 1962. The depot became famous for being the home to other sheds' cast offs, including the N15x Remembrance Class and the Urie 'Arthurs'.

When steam was officially banished from the Western Region in January 1966, the changeover point for Western-Southern traction became Basingstoke instead of Oxford. The line to Birmingham and the Midlands, however, now transferred to Midland Region control. This led to the regular appearance of former LMS Black 5s on inter-regional trains, supplemented by 8F and BR Standard 9Fs. The Southern engine crews at Basingstoke and Bournemouth immediately took a liking to the Black 5s and were reluctant to return them to their rightful homes. This was so much so that quite often borrowed Black 5s could be seen racing through Basingstoke on Bournemouth–Waterloo services at weekends.

Basingstoke Shed was always worth a visit when passing, for one never knew what might turn up. If one ever wanted to find out what, if anything, special was going on at Basingstoke, then the best person to speak to was old Ben Nash, the firelighter. Ben was always helpful to enthusiasts and would tip them off should anything unusual or special be happening. On 17 March 1966, BR Standard 3 No. 77014 was on shed while on its long journey south from Cheshire to a new home at Guildford. A few days later, on 25 March 1966, the LNER A4 60024 *Kingfisher* arrived on shed from Banbury with a freight en route to Nine Elms, ready to work the A4 Locomotive Society and LCGB rail tours. A Guildford Shed footplate crew (driver Alan Gaff and fireman Dick Bullen) took over the controls from Basingstoke to Nine Elms. On 30 June 1966, Basingstoke Shed welcomed another LNER visitor in the shape of V2 2-6-2 No. 60919. She arrived from her home shed of Dundee en route to Nine

Elms to work the Green Arrow rail tour on 3 July. Her condition was very poor and consequently she was failed at Nine Elms Shed. Despite valiant efforts with running repairs at Nine Elms and Eastleigh, she gave up the ghost at Basingstoke on the day of the special and was unceremoniously dumped at Basingstoke, much to the disappointment of enthusiasts.

Alan Pegler's preserved No. 4472 *Flying Scotsman* was serviced at Basingstoke on 10 September 1966 after hauling the Gainsborough Model Railway Society 'Farnborough Flyer' special train. Her appearance at Basingstoke attracted crowds of photographers, enthusiasts and dozens of local children. This sudden appearance of vast numbers of uninvited guests was a great cause of concern to shed staff, still busy attending to the needs of operating service locomotives for the Waterloo–Basingstoke semi-fasts.

Basingstoke was also a fascinating place in the context of railway signalling. This was radically to change with the Waterloo–Bournemouth electrification. The idea of the twenty-first-century power signal box, working hundreds of miles of signalling from a panel, is not a new one. The LSWR introduced a pneumatic system to operate points and signals between Woking and Basingstoke in the early 1900s. This successful signalling system was replaced in 1966. If permission could be obtained, a visit to the sixty-lever Basingstoke A signal box was well worth a look to view the strange looking 17in levers, which were mounted on a shelf at waist height. These levers were easily operated by simple pulls and pushes – an efficient and innovative system, which was to soon be replaced by new colour light signalling.

A beautifully clean rebuilt Merchant Navy Class No. 35018 *British India Line*, hauling the down *Bournemouth Belle* Pullman train, sails effortlessly under the lower quadrant signal gantry near Hook on 1 July 1961. (Britton Collection)

Breakfast on board the Waterloo–Southampton Docks boat train as it travels to meet the Cunard RMS *Mauretania* on 27 October 1964. (Valero Energy/Texaco)

Schools Class 4-4-0 No. 30902 *Wellington* is pictured heading a down Lymington Pier train into Basingstoke in the summer of 1959. Basingstoke shed received an allocation of displaced Schools Class from the eastern section following its electrification. The last three Schools Class were withdrawn from Basingstoke in 1962, but No. 30934 *St Lawrence* lingered in storage until she finally departed in steam on 18 May 1963, towing the last Drummond 700 Class down to Eastleigh for cutting up – a very sad occasion. (Britton Collection)

Q1 Class 0-6-0 No. 33021. The Q1 Class were affectionately known by railway crews and enthusiasts as 'Charlies'. Here an Eastleigh Shed crew, complete with their traditional railway tea cans, patiently wait to relieve a footplate crew from Guildford Shed. (Britton Collection)

A smart-looking rebuilt Bulleid West Country No. 34047 *Callington* makes a sure-footed departure from Basingstoke with the re-routed *Pines Express* in September 1964. (Britton Collection)

Variety and action at Basingstoke Shed on 18 July 1962 with Urie S15 4-6-0 No. 30514 and Schools Class 4-4-0 No. 30921 *Shrewsbury* flanked by a Maunsell 2-6-0, *left*, and a Maunsell S15 4-6-0, *right*. (David Cobbe/Britton Collection)

Engines amongst the ashes. By 17 September 1966 BR Standard designs dominated the scene at Basingstoke Shed with Standard 4 tank Nos 80151, 73037 and 76063 in the background. There was a feeling of run-down neglect by this stage, with filthy engines minus their smoke boxes and door numbers, and ash and debris scattered on the shed floor. (Britton Collection)

The visit to Basingstoke Shed of Alan Pegler's preserved LNER A3 No. 4472 *Flying Scotsman* on 10 September 1966 attracted photographers and enthusiasts from far and wide. It was standing room only to view the celebrity visitor. The contrast in appearance with the run-down Southern Region operating locomotives in the shed was quite noticeable. (Britton Collection)

Drummond 700 Class 0-6-0 No. 30368, complete with snow plough and Christmas tree growing out of its chimney, on 11 February 1962. (Britton Collection)

8

BASINGSTOKE TO MICHELDEVER

As the train leaves Basingstoke it passes the historic eleventh-century ruins of the chapels of Holy Ghost and Holy Trinity. Both are visible to the right. The burial ground on Chapel Hill dates from the period of the Interdict, when King John and all of England was excommunicated by the Pope and burials could not take place in consecrated ground. The excommunication was lifted after six years in 1214, and the cemetery was then consecrated and a chapel, dedicated to the Holy Ghost, was built. The thirteenth-century building was greatly enlarged in 1524 by Lord Sandys of The Vyne, when he added the Chapel of the Holy Trinity to the south side of the chancel.

West of Basingstoke is Worting Junction, where the Bournemouth and Salisbury lines diverged. Battledown Flyover acted as a magnet attracting steam enthusiasts and photographers from all over the country. Here the up Bournemouth line crossed the Salisbury–Exeter line using the impressive Battledown Flyover, which was built in 1897. Track widening was completed in 1904 to provide four tracks throughout to Waterloo. In 1963 administration of the line to Exeter beyond Salisbury was transferred to the Western Region. Sadly, this route was downgraded to a secondary line and singled in part. Shortly afterwards the crack express on the Exeter line, the *Atlantic Coast Express*, was banished. Regular steam working west of Salisbury became rare, but at Worting Junction steam could still be seen on Salisbury services until almost the end in 1967.

For the next 16 miles the railway descends past Steventon through tunnels and chalk cuttings over what was considered by steam locomotive crews as a racing ground, especially during the final few months of steam traction, when crews tried hard to achieve the 'magic ton'. The first of the tunnels is the 198yd Lichfield Tunnel, followed by the 265yd Popham Number 1 Tunnel, and 199yd Popham Number 2 Tunnel.

The railway now enters Micheldever over the River Dever, which is a 'winter bourne', i.e. a chalk stream that disappears during the summer through lack of replenishment, evaporation and the porous nature of the bedrock. The station itself was originally called Andover Road, until Andover got its own station. Unusually the station is a flint building with an added veranda. Just prior to electrification of the line in July 1967 the track layout was changed when the two side platforms were replaced by an island platform between the tracks. For many years the station sidings and storage sheds became the dumping ground for carriages and wagons awaiting repair at Eastleigh Works. In the mid-1960s Micheldever was the secret temporary home to redundant London Transport tube stock awaiting transfer to the Isle of Wight's Ryde–Shanklin line.

Micheldever Station was the starting point for the first automobile journey in Britain, in 1895. The vehicle, a Daimler-engined Panhard-Levassor, had been ordered from France by the Honourable Evelyn Ellis and was transported across the Channel by ferry and then to Micheldever Station by a LSWR train. The Honourable Evelyn Ellis received delivery on the platform and drove the car to Datchet, to deliberately test an Act of Parliament that required all self-propelled vehicles on public roads to travel at no more than 4mph, and to be preceded by a man waving a red flag. Significantly Ellis was not arrested and the Act was repealed in 1896, which opened up new possibilities for motoring in this country.

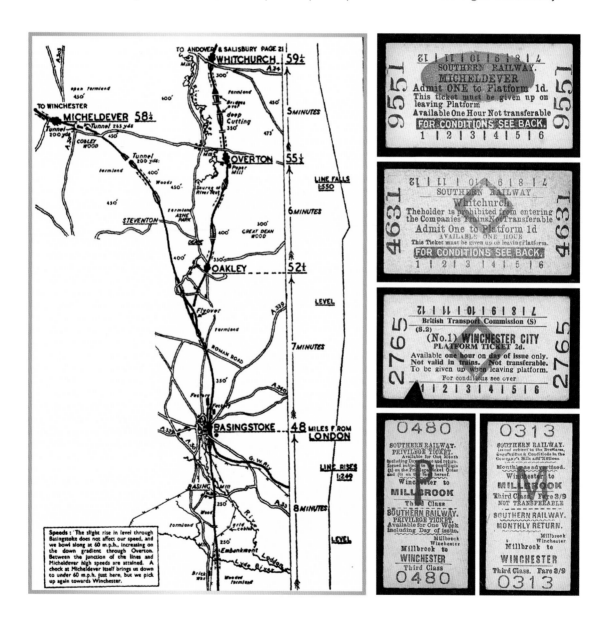

Rebuilt Merchant Navy Class No. 35027 *Port Line*, hauling the *Bournemouth Belle* Pullman train, races past Worting Junction signal box on 12 June 1964. (Bryan Hicks)

Looking across the freshly cut summer cornfield, we see the Schools Class 4-4-0 No. 30909 *St Paul's* racing over Battledown towards Basingstoke with a train from Lymington Pier on 8 August 1959. (Britton Collection)

Bulleid West Country Class No. 34099 *Lynmouth* burrows under Battledown Flyover with an up van train for Basingstoke and the capital. (Alan Sainty Collection)

Nine Elms driver Jim 'Robbo' Robinson opens up the regulator of the preserved A4 Pacific No. 4498 *Sir Nigel Gresley* at Worting Junction whilst heading for Bournemouth and Weymouth with a special on 4 June 1967. (Bryan Hicks)

BR Standard Class 4 No. 76066 charges out of the 198yd Lichfield Tunnel with a very short Clapham Junction to Eastleigh parcels train on 6 July 1967. She was working south to Weymouth to join the dumped engines at Weymouth, just days before the end of steam on the Southern. (Bryan Hicks)

Rebuilt West Country Class No. 34044 *Woolacombe* dashes past, hauling an up express, climbing away from the north end of Popham Tunnels on 1 August 1964. (David Peters)

9

MICHELDEVER TO WINCHESTER

Continuing from Micheldever the line descends through a deep cutting and into the 501yd Wallers Ash Tunnel before emerging into another deep cutting. Before entering Winchester the train passes the sight of the junction for the Watercress Line to Alton and over the former Great Western Winchester, Didcot & Newbury line. The line now closely follows the Itchen Valley. The River Itchen to the left of the train is said to be one of the finest fishing rivers in the country with bountiful supplies of brown trout, which command high prices for the privilege of fishing.

The train runs through a short cutting and under the old A34 road before the ancient city of Winchester presents itself to the passenger from the carriage window. Chalk hills rise above the city on both sides of the line. The 220ft summit of St Catherine's Hill can be seen to the south-east. The hill is owned by Winchester College but is managed as a nature reserve by Hampshire Wildlife Trust and is ringed by the ramparts of an Iron Age hill fort. The roof of the cathedral can also be seen on the left of the train. It is one of the largest cathedrals in England, and it has the longest nave and greatest overall length of any Gothic cathedral in Europe. It is dedicated to the Holy Spirit, St Peter, St Paul and St Swithun and is the seat of the Bishop of Winchester. The cathedral is the last resting place for many distinguished persons, including St Swithun, Izaak Walton and the English novelist Jane Austen. It is also the burial place of two of the four Danish kings of England: King Canute and his son Harthacanute. The last monarch to be buried in the city was the Norman King William II (William Rufus) who was killed while hunting in the New Forest.

Winchester's fame was established in the ninth century when King Alfred made the city England's first capital, which it continued to be until the Norman Conquest. Many visitors to Winchester make straight for the fine statue of King Alfred near the Guildhall. However, Winchester's hidden gem hangs on the wall in the Great Hall – the Great Round Table. According to legend, the Round Table is the table around which King Arthur and his Knights of the Round Table met, and it has been famous for centuries for its associations with the legendary 'Once and Future King'. The origins of the table lay many centuries later, but the table's mystique still remains. The Round Table was probably created in about 1290, for a tournament near Winchester to celebrate the betrothal of one of King Edward I's daughters. When the table was temporarily removed from the wall for inspection and investigated by a team of scientists in 1976, tree-ring evidence and carbon dating placed it in the thirteenth or early fourteenth century.

To the railway enthusiast, the city of Winchester is steeped in history. At one time there were two railway stations, Winchester City on the Southern and Winchester Chesil on the Western. The platform of the Southern station was an interesting place to watch fast trains like the *Bournemouth Belle* and the boat trains to Southampton Docks scream through, but the *Royal Wessex* was a regular stopper. A small engine shed was built by the Southern Railway in 1927. This was the home to a diminutive B4 0-4-0 tank engine. The affectionate nickname of the 'Flying Flea' for the Adams-designed 33-ton B4 tanks at Winchester originated from their ability to accelerate rapidly in short bursts. Most of the Waterloo–Bournemouth–Weymouth expresses stopped at Winchester. The Flying Flea was the station pilot engine and had the frequent task of attaching or detaching parcel vans. They literally jumped from siding to platform. The regular Winchester driver of the B4 'Flying Flea' was a very warm-hearted man who was partially disabled, but as he often said: 'I know the moods of the "Flying Flea" better than those of my wife.' This old driver was a remarkable fountain of information and revealed that the B4s had a tractive effort of 14,650lb with a boiler pressure of 140lb/in² and 3ft 9¾in driving wheels. 'The Flea' was withdrawn in 1963 to be exiled to Dibbles Wharf, Southampton, before being preserved at the Bluebell Railway in Sussex.

The Western station was opened with the line from Newbury on 4 May 1885, originally being named Winchester Cheesehill, but was renamed to Winchester Chesil on 26 September 1949. Chesil Station closed on 7 March 1960 but was reopened on Saturdays only for the next two summers: 18 June 1960 to 10 September 1960 and 17 June 1961 to 9 September 1961. The line remained busy after closure with freight services and Fawley oil tanker trains to the Midlands, but goods facilities were withdrawn from 4 April 1966.

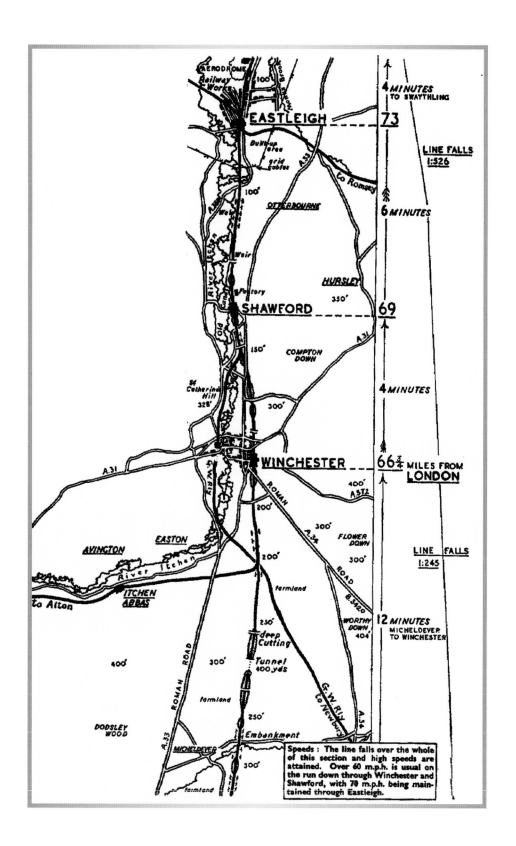

Speeds : The line falls over the whole of this section and high speeds are attained. Over 60 m.p.h. is usual on the run down through Winchester and Shawford, with 70 m.p.h. being maintained through Eastleigh.

A curious sight was captured through the lens of photographer Bryan Hicks at Micheldever Station on 12 June 1964, as S15 Class No. 30830 hauled a mixed freight to Eastleigh. Immediately behind the locomotive tender is a diesel shunter from Feltham, which is en route to Eastleigh Works for overhaul. (Bryan Hicks)

Rebuilt West Country Class No. 34021 *Dartmoor*, minus her nameplates, gallops away from Micheldever with a Bournemouth train on 3 June 1967. (Bryan Hicks)

With the third rail electrification programme in progress at Winchester, rebuilt Bulleid Light Pacific No. 34087 *145 Squadron* restarts her up semi-fast train to Waterloo on 3 September 1966. (Britton Collection)

At Winchester City Station on 30 June 1967, on the 8.35 a.m. from Waterloo, the footplate crew of rebuilt Merchant Navy Class No. 35023 *Holland Africa Line* are hard at work, topping up the water and breaking large lumps of coal in the tender. The safety valves are lifting and the Pacific appears to have a good head of steam. (Britton Collection)

BR Standard 5 4-6-0 No. 73022 trundles through Winchester City Station with a fitted freight from Southampton Docks in June 1966. (Britton Collection)

Winchester's 'Flying Flea' B4 tank No. 30102 in action. The affectionate nickname of the 'Flying Flea' originated from its ability to accelerate rapidly in short bursts. (Britton Collection)

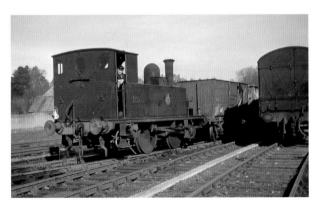

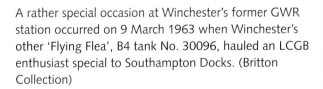

A rather special occasion at Winchester's former GWR station occurred on 9 March 1963 when Winchester's other 'Flying Flea', B4 tank No. 30096, hauled an LCGB enthusiast special to Southampton Docks. (Britton Collection)

10

WINCHESTER TO EASTLEIGH

Leaving Winchester, the River Itchen is seen gently flowing on the left of the train. The line passes the site of Shawford Junction, which took the Western line to Winchester Chesil and Newbury. Peering through the trees it is possible to look back and glimpse the abandoned but magnificent thirty-three-span GWR brick-built Hockley Viaduct. Although it appears to be a brick structure, the viaduct in fact has a solid concrete core in its pillars, with the bricks simply performing an aesthetic function, making it among the earliest modern structures to have a solid concrete core.

Passing under the new M3 motorway, which controversially sliced through the deep cutting at Twyford Down, the line now passes through Shawford Station, which has three platforms – two in the down direction. The railway continues to descend at a gradient of 1 in 526 to Allbrook Junction, north of Eastleigh, where the line to Romsey joins the main line on the right. From here rows of sidings dominated the landscape on the approach to Eastleigh. During the preparations for D-Day in 1944 they were packed from end to end with trains carrying tanks, guns and military equipment. Today the sidings are a mere shadow of their former glory and are sparsely used for engineering trains.

Eastleigh Station was originally opened as Bishopstoke and was built in 1839 to serve the junctions with the lines to Gosport, Portsmouth and Salisbury. In 1890 the London & South Western Railway progressively transferred its carriage works to Eastleigh. This was followed in 1909 by the construction of the Locomotive Works under the control of Dugald Drummond. When opened, the Locomotive Works employed 1,100 men, this along with the Carriage Works' 1,500 employees, made the railway the biggest employer of people in the area. Moreover, the LSWR built housing for their employees in Campbell Road and the surrounding streets. The town quickly established itself as a 'railway town' such as the likes of Crewe and Swindon. Eastleigh became the pride of the Southern Railway.

Eastleigh is 6 miles north of Southampton. To the railway enthusiast it was a key strategic railway centre with not only the main former LSWR main line from London–Southampton–Bournemouth and Weymouth running through, but also the junction for the Portsmouth and Salisbury lines. In addition to the running lines, Eastleigh acted as a magnet attracting railway enthusiasts to the works and running shed. Eastleigh depot (shed code 71A 1950 to 1963 and 70D 1963 to 1967) consisted of a ten-road through shed, which was capable of housing a substantial number of locomotives under cover. Shortly after nationalisation, the shed roof and gable ends were reclad in the distinctive corrugated asbestos sheeting. The shed was a perfect wind tunnel and could be a very cold and drafty place – summer or winter. Inside the shed fitters were provided with cube-shaped cast-iron braziers to keep them warm. At times, when the wind gusted, they erupted with golden sparks like the volcano Krakatoa! The shed was provided with a 55ft turntable on the north-east side of the shed and a turning triangle at the south side at the rear of the shed. Engines were coaled and watered around the clock and it is surprising that a Nine Elms-type coal hopper was not provided. A mechanical moving belt-type coaler was provided, but even so it meant many hours of unseen back-breaking sweat for those unsung heroes inside the coal stage.

The depot covered a wide network of operating passenger and freight diagrams to Salisbury, Bournemouth, Weymouth, Portsmouth, Reading, Oxford, Feltham, Waterloo and Brighton. Additionally, there were many shunting duties covered by lower links in the yards at Eastleigh, Northam, Bevois Park, Southampton Terminus and the Docks, Millbrook, Winchester, Romsey and Brockenhurst. The flagship workings were without doubt the Southampton Docks–Waterloo ocean liner boat trains, which were often worked by Lord Nelsons and Bulleid Light Pacifics. Eastleigh prided itself on the condition of its engines until the final few years of steam, when cleaners were less evident. It remained a stronghold of steam until closure at the end of SR steam in July 1967.

A visit to the running shed was always a great pleasure for railway enthusiasts. One was guaranteed to see Southern engines from right across the region, as many were awaiting transfer to the neighbouring works for overhaul and in latter days scrapping. Visiting engines from all regions could be seen on occasion. Western Region engines were regular visitors via the Winchester–Didcot–Newbury line and even a few Castles strayed in (and were impounded as a prohibited class) from the Salisbury line. Indeed, in June 1962, enthusiasts were astonished to see the now preserved double-chimney Castle Class 5043 *Earl of Mount Edgcumbe* on shed. Apparently this Castle had been removed from a Portsmouth-bound excursion by the Eastleigh's Motive Power Superintendent, Mr Townroe. She was isolated with strict instructions 'not to be moved owing to gauging restrictions!' Hall, Grange and Manor 4-6-0s were a common sight on the main line, working through trains to Bournemouth West. Likewise, the 10xx County Class 4-6-0s made frequent appearances on excursion trains. Western 28xx and 43xx classes were also regular visitors with freights to the Docks. Midland Region: Stanier Black Fives, 8Fs, Jubilees, Patriots, Royal Scots and Flying Pigs were also spotted on shed on occasion. The LNER A4 60024 *Kingfisher* and A3 *Flying Scotsman* even visited Eastleigh for servicing when working enthusiast excursions.

In latter days BR Standard classes seemed to dominate Eastleigh Shed. The depot had an allocation of 9Fs, which were used on Fawley–Bromford Bridge oil tanker trains until 1963. Standard 4 75xxx and 76xxx 4-6-0s were in daily use on semi-fast and local stopping trains. Standard 4MT 80xxx tanks were also in common use locally, working passenger and freight traffic. The Standard locomotives proved to be popular and reliable with Eastleigh crews. In fact, many Eastleigh enginemen have openly stated that they preferred a Standard 5 73xxx to a Bulleid Pacific when working ocean liner boat expresses.

Each winter a reliable and free-steaming Eastleigh 0-6-0 engine would be set aside for 'special duties'. Sometimes it was a Drummond Black Motor 700 Class. In latter days a Maunsell Q Class was allocated. This locomotive was the most important engine on the depot and the 'special duties' meant that the selected engine was always kept with a full tender of coal, well lubricated with oil and checked over daily. What was this special duty? The snow plough engine! In anticipation of inclement weather the selected engine would have her front buffers removed and the snow plough bolted on in place. I recall in the severe winter of 1962/63 the snow-plough-fitted Q Class 30535 was the most popular and petted engine at Eastleigh.

Tucked away at Eastleigh was another vital piece of railway equipment, DS35, the motive power depot 36-ton steam-boilered breakdown crane. The crane and match truck were regularly checked and maintained in 'ship shape and Bristol fashion' for immediate twenty-four-hour call up. The Ransom-and-Rapier-built crane was permanently attached to two departmental carriages, which were equipped with a mobile kitchen. It was the practice at Eastleigh for any available engine to be used to haul the brake down train whenever the services of the Brake Down Gang were required in a hurry.

Visits to the works were always restricted to Works open days. This would be a family outing lasting all afternoon. It was possible at the open days to clamber all over the pristine ex-works engines and explore the erecting shops, fitting and millwrights shop, boiler repair shop, weighbridge and paint shop. I never ceased to be amazed at the sight of stripped-down engines propped up on support jacks or Bulleid Pacifics in the process of modification to their new rebuilt condition. Huge tools littered the floor or were stored on workbenches. Odd boxpok Bulleid bogies and spoked driving wheels lay around with white chalk marking on the flanges. Overhead mobile cranes on gantries rested waiting for the return of the workforce the following Monday morning.

During the Second World War nearly a third of the work was given over to military supplies. This included the conversion of Blenheim bombers into fighters, component production of Spitfires, landing craft assembly and caterpillar track production for tanks. This vital wartime work attracted frequent unwelcome raids from the German Luftwaffe and anti-aircraft batteries were strategically positioned around the perimeter.

As steam traction began to disappear in the early 1960s, opportunities presented themselves to purchase locomotive souvenirs at works' open days. A rack would be assembled and a collection of brass nameplates from withdrawn locomotives would be displayed priced at £5 per nameplate! Next door to this was a table with further bargains, including the accompanying smoke box door number plates and locomotive whistles. Oh, if only one had saved pocket money for this occasion! At the back of the works long lines of withdrawn engines waited the cutter's torch. Visitors could stray away from the crowds visiting the open day to pay their last respects to lines of Schools Class and cab them all for a final time.

From March 1964 Eastleigh Works began overhauling Midland Region steam locomotives. Ivatt Flying Pig 2-6-0s and foreign Standard 4 75xxx engines were out-shopped and run in on the locals. They were joined by London Transport Pannier tanks and blue-liveried military-owned engines. If memory serves me correctly, I even saw the National Collection's preserved Western Region 28xx Class outside the works resplendent in Eastleigh green livery! The last steam locomotive repair at Eastleigh Works was to 34089 *602 Squadron* in October 1966 and was recorded by the local BBC Television's *South Today*.

Back at the running shed all remained steamy up to the beginning of 1966. The then allocation of sixty-seven steam locomotives included twenty-six Bulleid Pacifics, but from this date on steam was in full retreat. During the last week of steam in 1967 it was so sad to see the Eastleigh allocation of steam engines slip away into storage at Salisbury MPD and thence to the scrapyards of South Wales. Fittingly, it was at Eastleigh's Campbell Road Bridge that many devotees watched the last up steam working to Waterloo on the Southern with Merchant Navy 35030 *Elder Dempster Lines* on the 2.07 p.m. from Weymouth in July 1967.

Eastleigh Works Open Day 1962, with hundreds of visitors in attendance. The highlight of the open day was the unveiling of the freshly out-shopped Drummond T9 30120, which had received a heavy casual overhaul and returned to active service in LSWR green as No. 120. Visitors were able to climb up onto the footplates of all the locomotives on display, which included a rebuilt Merchant Navy Class, un-rebuilt West Country Class, a BR Standard Class 4 tank, a Class 33 Crompton diesel and an electro-diesel. What would the Health & Safety officials of today say about young children climbing on the tender tops, cabs and boilers of steam locomotives? (Britton Collection)

Crowds of admirers pour in to scramble all over the freshly overhauled steam locomotives on display the open day. Amongst them is author Andrew Britton on the front step of BR Standard Class 5 No. 73029, with his sister Ruth and their mother standing alongside. (Britton Collection)

LSWR 4-4-0 T3 Class No. 563, designed by William Adams and built in 1893, stands beside Eastleigh Works awaiting entry for cosmetic restoration and a fresh coat of paint. She will then be transported to Clapham Transport Museum. Today this preserved engine is part of the National Collection and is exhibited in the National Railway Museum at York. (Britton Collection)

The ex-Eastleigh Works Terrier tank No. 32678 has just emerged from the paint shops in British Railways' lined black livery and with a spark arrestor on her Drummond chimney. After starting her career on the Isle of Wight branch lines in the 1930s, she was renumbered and named by the Southern Railway *13 Bembridge* and fitted with an extended coal bunker. She returned to the mainland and for many years worked on the Hayling Island line. Closure of the branch finally ended her BR career and in 1964 she was sold to Butlins, becoming an exhibit in the playground at Minehead. Today she is based on the Kent & East Sussex Railway and is an occasional guest at enthusiast galas. (Britton Collection)

Inside Eastleigh Works, B4 tank No. 30102 is receiving a major overhaul. This 0-4-0 tank engine saw regular service at Winchester where she was known as the 'Flying Flea'. The B4 tanks were introduced in 1891 by the London South Western Railway for shunting in Southampton Docks. After replacement by the heavier USA tanks during the Second World War, the B4s found new employment as shed pilot locomotives and at Winchester yard. Happily, No. 30102 escaped the scrap merchant's torch and is now preserved at Bressingham. (Britton Collection)

The gigantic Urie H16 4-6-2 tank No. 30517 is pictured undergoing a major overhaul in the depths of Eastleigh Works. She has had her wheels removed for the fitting of new tyres and re-profiling, a cylinder re-bore is under way, with a complete boiler re-tube. After a few weeks in the shops, the locomotive returned to service at Feltham Shed completely repainted and looking immaculate. (Britton Collection)

Peering over the fence into Eastleigh Works was a major attraction for railway enthusiasts in steam days as it was possible to view which locomotives were about to enter the shops for overhaul. Here, preserved Drummond M7 No. 30053 and an unidentified Bulleid Pacific await their turn in the works queue. This view was taken on a Sunday morning, as the workforce bicycle sheds are completely empty. (Britton Collection)

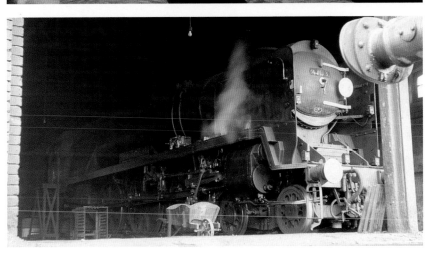

This evocative picture captures the real atmosphere of Eastleigh Shed towards the end of the steam era and shows rebuilt West Country Class No. 34104 *Bere Alston* undergoing routine maintenance. Note the typical wooden wheelbarrow used by shed fitters and the smoke box of the engine minus her number and shed plates. (Britton Collection)

Eastleigh Locomotive and Carriage Works
OPEN DAY
WEDNESDAY, AUGUST 5th
COMBINED RAIL AND ADMISSION TICKETS

FROM	DEPART	RETURN FARES (2nd class) including admission to Works	FROM	DEPART	RETURN FARES (2nd class) including admission to Works
		s. d.			s. d.
WATERLOO	11R30 a.m.	11/-	MICHELDEVER	12.51 p.m.	4/-
ALDERSHOT	12A27 a.m.	6/6	MOTTISFONT	1.12 p.m.	3/6
ALRESFORD	1.9 p.m.	4/-	NETLEY	12C27, 1C15 p.m.	3/-
ALTON	12.53 p.m.		NEW MILTON	11.27 a.m. & 1.36 p.m.	7/6
ANDOVER JUNCT.	12.42 p.m.	5/-	NORTHAM	12.55, 1.27 p.m.	2/5
ANDOVER TOWN	12.45 p.m.	4/9	POKESDOWN	11.11 a.m. & 1.19 p.m.	7/-
BASINGSTOKE	12R29, 12.34 p.m.	5/-	POOLE	12N24 p.m.	8/3
BEDHAMPTON HALT	12B36 p.m.	4/9	PORTCHESTER	1.2 p.m.	3/9
BOGNOR REGIS	11H36 a.m.	6/9	PORTSMOUTH &		
BOSCOMBE	11.8 a.m. & 1.16 p.m.	7/-	SOUTHSEA	12.43 p.m.	4/6
BOTLEY	1.24 p.m.	2/6	RINGWOOD	11J9 a.m. & 1J11 p.m.	6/6
BOURNEMOUTH			ROMSEY	1.19 p.m.	2/10
CENTRAL	11.5 a.m., 12N40, 1.10 p.m.	7/9	ROPLEY	1.5 p.m.	4/3
BRIGHTON	10B17, 11B17 a.m.	10/-	RYDE ESPLANADE	10F18, 11F18 a.m.	7/6
BROCKENHURST	12.40, & 1.51 p.m.	4/6	RYDE PIER HEAD	10F30, 11F30 a.m.	7/9
CHICHESTER	12B7, 12P19 p.m.	5/6	ST. DENY'S	12.58, & 1.30 p.m.	2/2
CHRISTCHURCH	11.16 a.m. & 1.24 p.m.	6/3	SALISBURY	12K42 p.m.	5/-
CLATFORD	12.49 p.m.	4/9	SHOREHAM-BY-SEA	10B27, 11B27 a.m.	9/6
CORFE CASTLE	11.50 a.m.	9/9	SOUTHAMPTON		
COSHAM	12.55 p.m.	4/-	CENTRAL	12.8, 1.25, 2.15 p.m.	2/5
DEAN	12K56 p.m.	3/9	SOUTHAMPTON		
DILTON MARSH			TERMINUS	12.25, 12.53, 1.25 p.m.	
HALT	11M50 a.m.	7/-	STOCKBRIDGE	1.1 p.m.	4/9
DORCHESTER			SUTTON SCOTNEY	1.7 p.m.	3/9
SOUTH	11N47 a.m.	10/9	SWANAGE	11N40 a.m.	10/-
DUNBRIDGE	1K2 p.m.	3/6	SWANWICK	1C6 p.m.	3/-
FAREHAM	1.8 p.m.	3/6	SWAYTHLING	12.33, 1.1, 1.33 p.m.	1/10
FARNHAM	12A33 p.m.	6/9	TOTTON	11.59 a.m.	3/-
FLEET	11D51 a.m.	6/3	WAREHAM	12N12 p.m.	9/-
FRATTON	12.46 p.m.	4/3	WARMINSTER	12M1 p.m.	6/6
FULLERTON	12.55 p.m.	4/9	WEST MOORS	10J57 a.m., 1J1 p.m.	7/-
HAVANT	12B27, 12B34 p.m.	4/9	WEST WORTHING	10B36, 11B36 a.m.	9/-
HORSEBRIDGE	1.7 p.m.	10/6	WEYMOUTH	11N30 a.m.	11/9
HORSHAM	10B15, 11B15 a.m.	9/9	WHITCHURCH		
HOVE	10B20, 11B20 a.m.	9/9	TOWN	12.56 p.m.	4/3
ITCHEN ABBAS	1.14 p.m.	3/6	WINCHESTER CITY	12.55, 1.6, 1.23 p.m.	2/9
LITTLEHAMPTON	11E46 a.m.	7/-	WOKING	11D27 a.m., 12A9 p.m.	8/-
LYNDHURST ROAD	11.52 a.m.	3/6	WOOLSTON	12C32, 1C21 p.m.	2/9
MEDSTEAD &			WORTHING		
FOURMARKS	1.1 p.m.	4/9	CENTRAL	10B34, 11B34 a.m.	9/-

A—Change at Alton. B—Change at Fratton. D—Change at Basingstoke. E—Change at Ford and Fratton. F—Change at Portsmouth Harbour and Portsmouth and Southsea. H—Change at Barnham and Fratton. J—Change at Brockenhurst. K—Change at Romsey. L—Change at Wareham and Southampton Central. M—Change at Salisbury and Romsey. N—Change at Southampton Central. P—Change at Fareham.

R—Restaurant Car.

CHILDREN UNDER 14 YEARS HALF FARE
Children under 5 years not admitted into Works

→ **RETURN BY ANY TRAIN SAME DAY** ←
including the following additional trains:—

EASTLEIGH depart 4.55 p.m. to Southampton Central (change for Totton and Lyndhurst Road), Brockenhurst, New Milton, Christchurch, Pokesdown, Boscombe and Bournemouth Central.
EASTLEIGH depart 5.0 p.m. to Fareham, Cosham and Fratton.
EASTLEIGH depart 4.55 p.m. to Winchester City.

THE LOCOMOTIVE WORKS AND CARRIAGE AND WAGON WORKS
will be open to visitors from 1.30 p.m. to 4.30 p.m.
(Proceeds to Southern Railway Servants' Orphanage, Woking)
Light Refreshments will be obtainable in the works Canteen

Tickets may be obtained in advance at Stations or Travel Agencies

NOTICE AS TO CONDITIONS—These tickets are issued subject to the British Transport Commission's published Regulations and Conditions applicable to British Railways exhibited at their stations or obtainable free of charge at station booking offices

Waterloo Station, S.E.1 / A15
July, 1959 C.X.363/14759 (SOUTHERN)

Printed in Great Britain by
Stringer, Briggs, Stockley & Co., Kingston

II

EASTLEIGH TO SOUTHAMPTON

The line running out of Eastleigh runs parallel with the road on the right-hand side and enthusiastic lovers of steam in the 1960s could often be seen racing trains to film cine footage. On the opposite side is the airport's runway, which was built over the remains of a Roman villa. The site's connection with aviation can be traced back to 1910 when Edwin Rowland Moon used the North Stoneham Farm meadows as a take-off and landing point for his monoplane, *Moonbeam Mark II*.

During the final months of the First World War, the United States Navy was based on the site and constructed hangars. Some 4,000 officers and men were billeted in tents and temporary wooden huts adjacent the main railway line.

In 1932 Southampton Corporation purchased the site and renamed it Southampton Municipal Airport. The airport became famous on 5 March 1936 when the first test flight of R.J. Mitchell's Supermarine Spitfire took place. During the Second World War the airport was taken over by the Royal Navy and RAF. After the war, during the 1950s, the airport became a major departure point for the Channel Islands, with the famous Silver City Airways car-carrying Bristol Superfreighters, and the passenger-carrying Handley Page Herald and De Havilland Dove aircraft. In 1966 a new concrete runway was built to allow larger jet aircraft to fly out of Southampton.

A railway station was opened on the site next to the airport as the Atlantic Park Hostel Halt in 1929 but later closed. In 1966 a new station was built as Southampton Airport Halt, which changed its name in 1986 to Southampton Parkway, with another name change to Southampton Airport Parkway in the 1990s.

The next station, Swaythling, was built in 1883 and is of interest as it was built in a neo-Flemish style and is so architecturally important that it has a Grade 2 preservation order. The up side on the right-hand side of the train has a Flemish gable with central pediment and ball finials with a date tablet. The station has changed very little since it was opened.

The line through the Southampton suburbs is now level and runs into St Denys Station, which is the junction station for the Netley and Portsmouth line. Opened as Portswood, the station buildings are a fine example of Victorian architecture. The old station buildings on platform 4 are now the headquarters of the Solent Model Railway Group. Beyond the station are the once-busy Northam freight yards.

The remnants of Northam Station, which closed on 5 September 1966, can just be made out. This was the busy junction for trains heading to Southampton Terminus Station and the Docks past Mount Pleasant freight yards. At one time, many Ocean Liner Expresses ran non-stop from Waterloo to the Docks, with passengers for the Cunard Queen liners going to New York. To the left of the train can be seen the new St Mary's Football Stadium, which replaced The Dell as the home of Southampton Football Club.

The train now dramatically slows down at Northam Junction. Here the line parts with the original route to Southampton and snakes sharply right, crawling towards the former Tunnel Junction and under the lattice wrought-iron bridge carrying the Southampton–Portsmouth road, before entering the damp and claustrophobic 528yd Southampton Tunnel under the Civic Centre.

Trainspotting from Swaythling footbridge in the days of steam was always great fun. Here an unidentified rebuilt Bulleid Pacific rushes through with a southbound train, during the latter days of steam on the Southern in 1967. (Britton Collection)

During the electrification work of the Waterloo–Bournemouth line, trains were frequently diverted via Fareham and Petersfield or over the Mid-Hants Watercress Line. On 20 March 1966, rebuilt West Country Class No. 34032 *Camelford* on the 7.30 a.m. Waterloo to Bournemouth train followed the diversion route. It is seen here at Bursleden on the approach to rejoin the mainline at St Denys. Note the Watneys advertisement on the bridge and the Hillman Minx car on an almost empty road. (Britton Collection)

St Denys Station on 3 September 1966 sees rebuilt Merchant Navy Class No. 35013 *Blue Funnel* racing through with the *Bournemouth Belle*. (Britton Collection)

The Victorian terrace houses at Tunnel Junction in Northam make a fine backdrop to No. 31792 in this late 1950s picture. The tall Tunnel Junction signal box can be seen to the left of the train. (Alan Sainty Collection)

Closed and deserted platforms at Northam Station on 3 September 1966. (Britton Collection)

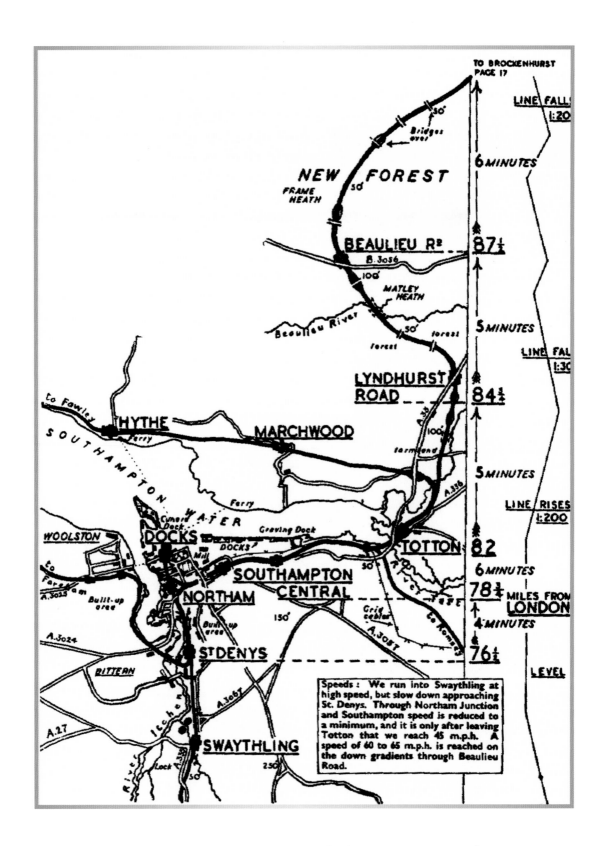

12

SOUTHAMPTON

Bursting out of the tunnel into daylight the train enters Southampton Central Station. The station was opened as Southampton West in 1895 and was on the seafront with tidal water reaching right up to the platform edges at high tide. The London & South Western Railway and later the Southern Railway funded a series of land reclamation projects, which culminated in the construction of the Western Docks in 1934. The new reclaimed land was drained and reinforced with granite to allow expansion and redevelopment of the station. The ornate station clock tower, which was a well-liked local landmark, was sadly knocked down prior to electrification in 1967 and replaced by a bland office block.

Southampton has been a seaport from the earliest times, though its importance in the modern sense began only 150 years ago. The heyday of the great liners lasted up to the late 1960s and coincided with the demise of steam on the railways. In those days Cunard operated a regular two-liner transatlantic service from Southampton to New York with RMS *Queen Mary* and RMS *Queen Elizabeth,* which at the time was the largest liner in the world. This service was rivalled by the streamlined Blue Riband holder for the fastest crossings of the Atlantic, SS *United States* and her sister SS *America.* A frequent visitor to the port of Southampton was the longest liner in the world, the French Line ship SS *France.* Visitors to Southampton could also see the glorious P&O liners *Oriana, Oronsay, Orsova* and *Canberra* sailing out to Australia and on cruises. There was also a weekly service to Cape Town in South Africa with the Union Castle Line. The port of Southampton, known as the Gateway to the World, was bustling with Red Funnel paddle steamers and ferries to the Isle of Wight, Red Funnel and Alexandra Towing tugs and gigantic flying boats heading off to the Mediterranean.

After taking water under the famous enormous signal gantry at the west end of Southampton Central Station, the train would leave the station, offering passengers a fine panoramic view on the left as it gathered speed through Millbrook and Redbridge stations. Today it is still possible to gain some impression of those former days with glimpses of the modern cruise liners and the gigantic container vessels when they are docked in Southampton. Sadly, the King George V Graving Dock, where many ocean liners were dry docked for their annual refit, has now gone. Looking left you will see two new enormous green container-handling cranes at Freightliner's Southampton

Maritime Terminal. These rail head gantry cranes, which straddle thirteen rail tracks, can lift thirty box containers an hour. The £9 million cranes were named 'Freightliner Fortis' and 'Freightliner Agilitas' and commissioned by the Mayor of Southampton and Freightliner's Managing Director in October 2012.

As the train passes through Redbridge, it is possible to see the remnants of the railway sleeper Works, which closed on 3 March 1989. The Redbridge Works had the capability of prefabricating on site entire junctions of railway point work and had a creosote plant for the preservation of new wooden railway sleepers. Trains would transport entire 60ft lengths of lines and new sleepers to all parts of the network across the south. British Rail changed its policy to outsource to private contractors, but the memory of the departmental USA tanks shunting heavy trains around the site lives on.

The train crosses the estuary of the River Test across Redbridge Causeway with a wonderful view of the marshland towards Eling's eighteenth-century tide mill, and on a clear day a good view of Southampton Water. A new bridge across the estuary was built towards the end of the steam era in the winter of 1963/64. Just before the A35 flyover bridge passengers will smell the distinctive aroma of the South Western Tar Distillery, which is always a relief to be well past.

The station at Totton was opened in 1847 as Eling Junction, which is the name of the junction with the Fawley branch to the west of the station. It was renamed in 1859 to the current name of Totton to serve what was claimed to be the largest village in England until made a town in 1974. The branch to Fawley closed to passengers on 14 February 1966, but continues to remain open for oil trains to the refinery. During the final years of steam traction the branch became a popular destination for enthusiast trains hauled by the USA dock shunters. The Fawley branch was known to many as the 'Silver City branch' referring to the vast oil storage tanks.

The up Weymouth–Waterloo *Channel Islands Boat Express*, hauled by rebuilt West Country Class No. 34032 *Camelford*, heads away from Southampton Central on 10 September 1966. (Britton Collection)

Southampton Central railway station, with West Country Class No. 34045 *Ottery St Mary*. The London Nine Elms Shed crew have just handed over the controls to a Bournemouth crew and seem oblivious to the smoking funnels of SS United States in the distance. (Norman Roberts/Britton Collection)

A brace of Bulleid Light Pacifics rest at Southampton Central on 20 August 1966. On the right in platform 1 is No. 34087 *145 Squadron* and on the left in platform 2 is No. 34005 *Barnstaple*. Behind is the 100ft clock tower erected in 1892 but sadly demolished later in 1966 prior to redevelopment of the site, which included a hideous, characterless modern five-storey concrete building. (Britton Collection)

BR Standard Class 4 No. 76064 crosses Canute Road in Southampton with a boat train for the docks during the last few days of steam. The train boards show that it is the *Ocean Liner Express*, which met the Cunard RMS *Queen Elizabeth* that was sailing for Cherbourg and New York. (David Peters)

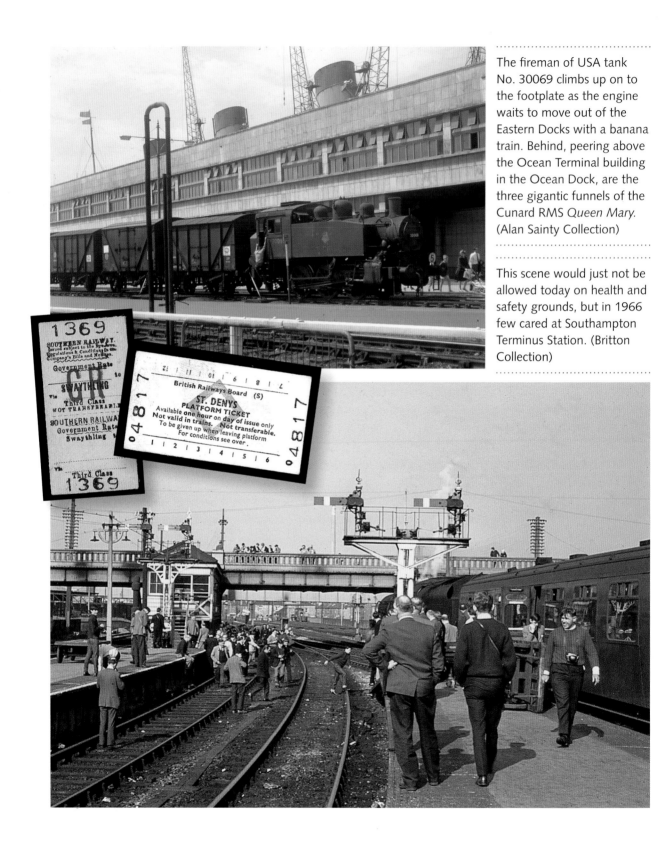

The fireman of USA tank No. 30069 climbs up on to the footplate as the engine waits to move out of the Eastern Docks with a banana train. Behind, peering above the Ocean Terminal building in the Ocean Dock, are the three gigantic funnels of the Cunard RMS *Queen Mary*. (Alan Sainty Collection)

This scene would just not be allowed today on health and safety grounds, but in 1966 few cared at Southampton Terminus Station. (Britton Collection)

Merchant Navy Class No. 35004 *Cunard White Star* was provided by Nine Elms locomotive shed in London to haul the *Mauretania* Regent Refinery Opening special train. A circular smoke box name board reading *Regent* was attached. The special train is pictured at Ocean Terminal Station in Southampton shortly after arrival. The engine has been polished to perfection for the occasion, which took place on 27 October 1964. (Valero Energy/ Texaco)

B4 tank No. 30096 in action at Dibbles Wharf in Southampton. Following withdrawal from service by British Railways she was sold to Corralls the coal merchants. (Britton Collection)

13

TOTTON TO BROCKENHURST

Leaving Totton the railway passes under Brokenford Bridge and enters the New Forest at Ashurst Crossing. After passing under the Ashurst Road Bridge the line sweeps around the curve to what was, in steam days, Lyndhurst Road Station, now renamed Ashurst New Forest Station. Although named Lyndhurst Road Station, it was actually some way from the village of Lyndhurst, which is the administrative capital of the New Forest. The station had its own unique charm in steam days with canopies, oil lamps on the platform and a covered footbridge. Next to the road bridge was a signal box where visitors were always welcome. Until 1965 the station boasted an umber and cream liveried camping coach called *Ruby* on the down side. This 1914 Pullman achieved fame on the cover of the 1963 BR Camping Coach booklet.

The railway line now heads through the trees of the New Forest past Deer Leap and through Churchplace and Longdown Inclosure. Observant passengers may be able to spot hidden deer among the pine trees. The railway is now on an embankment and crosses the Beaulieu river, Fulford Bog and Matley Heath. This was originally an area of thick forestation but was cleared for timbers for ship building at Bucklers Hard.

This beautiful heathland has a carpet of purple heather and the embankment is lined with yellow gorse in the spring. New Forest ponies can be seen roaming across the heathland and the peace is only broken by the sound of chattering curlews. At night (in the spring and summer) the heath becomes alive with night jars, owls and foraging badgers. During the steam era stray sparks from the chimneys of passing locomotives would often set the heath alight. The cutting on the climb to Beaulieu Road Station was until recently shrouded with pine trees on either side of the line. At night, during the summer months, it is the favourite habitat of the glow worm, which can be seen from the carriage window. Originally the pony sales were held in Lyndhurst, but when the railway was built the sale was relocated. Special sidings were provided on the down side of the station and ponies were transported to all parts of the network. These sidings have long since been removed. Until 1 June 1964, this lonely station boasted canopies, paraffin-lit platform lights and a manned ticket office. During the summer and autumn of 1966, between 31 July and 23 October, a temporary signal frame was installed for the preparation work for electrification with trains running single line to Brockenhurst.

Up until 1964, during the fortnight prior to Christmas each year, many Waterloo–Weymouth passenger and freight trains would unofficially stop at Beaulieu Road Station, including the *Bournemouth Belle* and *Royal Wessex*, but why was this many passengers wondered? The answer to this question may now be revealed. Footplate crews from Nine Elms, Guildford, Eastleigh and Bournemouth would unofficially briefly halt their express trains in the short platform and freshly cut New Forest Christmas trees for the footplate crews and train guards would be quickly loaded into the luggage compartment of the first coach! In return the station staff at Beaulieu Road received a constant supply of loco coal throughout the year for their fires from passing engines, making this little New Forest station the warmest on the Southern Region. Locally caught rabbits were also provided to passing train crews who exchanged them for fresh eggs and allotment-grown vegetables. Even bagged horse muck from the Beaulieu Road Pony Sales for railwaymen's rose gardens has been observed being loaded on top of the coal of the tenders of passing locomotives.

Beyond the station on the Bishop of Winchester's Purlieu was a huge Italian prisoner-of-war camp during the Second World War. The prisoners set about repairing Forest bridges and pathways, many of which remain to this day. The line sweeps around a sharp curve and descends into Denny Lodge Inclosure and on to Woodfidley Crossing and cottages. During the Second World War a special siding was installed for MOD timber recovery from the New Forest. The passenger on the train can gain an impression of the New Forest for the next few miles as trees line the railway line as the train races through Ladycross Inclosure towards Brockenhurst.

Upon entering Brockenhurst the landscape opens out as the train crosses the Lymington river and crosses the level crossing before entering the station. Brockenhurst Station was rebuilt in 1936 with two island platforms connected by a covered footbridge and is the most important station in the New Forest. It was the junction for the 'Old Road Castleman's Corkscrew line' to Holmsley, Ringwood, Wimborne and Broadstone, which closed in 1964. The other branch line to Lymington remains open. The station has an unusual luggage traverser bridge, which can be moved out over the track to provide access to platform 1 on the up side. At one time the station boasted its own turntable, where locomotives hauling through services from London could be turned and serviced. Additionally, the station had extensive sidings where carriage sets could be stored for weekend and holiday season services. During the 1950s and '60s, Brockenhurst was a hive of activity with Drummond M7 branch line push-pull services, numerous Maunsell Q Class and moguls and an abundance of British Railways Standard engines. To the trainspotter, Brockenhurst was an oasis. There were three signal boxes at Brockenhurst: A and B and Lymington Junction, which controlled the lines to Lymington and the 'Old Road'. All were closed when Eastleigh Panel Box came into operation, although a mini-panel replaced Brockenhurst A in operation of the level crossing.

Super power at Lyndhurst Road Station on 18 June 1967 as rebuilt Bulleid Light Pacifics Nos 34089 *602 Squadron* and 34108 *Wincanton* sweep around the curve with the RCTS 'Farewell to Southern Steam Rail Tour'. (Britton Collection)

Rebuilt West Country Class No. 34034 *Honiton* arrives into Lyndhurst Road Station with steam to spare blowing from the safety valves on 28 May 1966. (Gerald Robinson/Britton Collection)

A visit to the National Motor Museum at Beaulieu in the mid-1960s was always a great thrill, especially after Lord Montague of Beaulieu had the foresight to preserve a sample of the Southern Steam era by purchasing Schools Class No. 928 *Stowe* and three representative Pullman carriages of the *Bournemouth Belle.* The Schools Class now resides at the Bluebell Railway in Sussex. (Britton Collection)

Sunlight and shadows near Woodfidley Crossing between Beaulieu Road Station and Brockenhurst in the midst of the New Forest. Rebuilt Merchant Navy Class No. 35008 *Orient Line* sweeps around the curve with the down *Pines Express.* (John Cox)

A perfectly framed portrait of rebuilt Bulleid Light Pacific No. 34088 *213 Squadron* approaches Brockenhurst with the down *Bournemouth Belle* on 2 July 1966. (David Peters)

Smiles all round from the footplate crew of rebuilt West Country Class No. 34089 *602 Squadron*, which is about to depart with an up semi-fast for Southampton, Winchester, Basingstoke and Waterloo. (John Cox)

Brockenhurst had its own 50ft turntable where locomotives hauling through services from London could be turned and serviced. Here Schools Class No. 30906 *Sherborne* is being turned the hard way. (Alan Sainty Collection)

Polished to perfection with whitened buffers, Standard Class 4 tank No. 80151 pauses at Brockenhurst on 25 March 1967 whilst hauling the 'Hants & Dorset Branch Line Flyer' enthusiast special. (Britton Collection)

14

BROCKENHURST TO BOURNEMOUTH

From Brockenhurst the line heads out towards Lymington Junction. To the left the branch to Lymington heads away and immediately to the right are the remains of the formation of the track bed carrying the 'Old Road' line to Holmsley, Ringwood and Wimborne. Until 1964 holiday trains to Swanage and Weymouth would travel along the 'Old Road' and avoid the busy congestion of Bournemouth and Poole. The line also saw a lot of use as a diversion route when the main line via Sway was closed for engineering or track maintenance.

Leaving Lymington Junction the train crosses a skew bridge over the Sway road below. The local authorities refused to divert the road to accommodate the construction of the new railway when built by the LSWR. The line climbs at 1 in 103 and is carried on an embankment across Widden Bottom where New Forest ponies can be seen grazing. The route to Bournemouth via Sway is more direct than the 'Old Road' line but was not opened until 6 March 1888. Upon entering Sway it is impossible to see the village as the station is buried in a cutting. At Sway there were also two Pullman Camping Coaches: the 1914 Birmingham Carriage & Wagon Co. *Daphne* and the 1912 Cravens Ltd *Seville*. The name Sway originates from the Old English name *Svieia*, which means noisy stream. Sway is perhaps best known for the 200ft Sway Tower, also known as Peterson's Folly. This landmark on the local skyline, which can be seen for miles, is constructed entirely out of concrete made with Portland cement, with only the windows having iron supports. The Tower was erected by an eccentric barrister named Andrew Peterson who was trying to demonstrate the potential of concrete. It remains the tallest non-reinforced concrete structure in the world. Sway Tower was originally designed as a mausoleum with a perpetual light at the top, but this was not allowed by Trinity House as it was thought that the light would confuse shipping between Lymington and the Isle of Wight.

Heading west from Sway the line passes through a series of cuttings to New Milton. When built there was a lot of debate on what to call the new station. Milton was suggested, but there are a number of places with that name in England. Barton was also suggested, but discounted for the same reason. The name New Milton for the station came by accident as the local sub-post mistress called her new sub-post office across the road from the station New Milton and so the station name was agreed. The skyline at New Milton is dominated by a water tower designed in Tudor style and built in 1900. The line out of New Milton goes through more cuttings and the gradient falls at 1 in 253 before climbing up Walkford Bank to Hinton Admiral Station.

Hinton Admiral Station was once among the heath and woodland. Until 1965 it was the home for the 1914-built Cravens twelve-wheeled holiday coach Pullman *Hibernia*, which was transferred to Lyndhurst Road Station. Beyond Hinton Admiral Station on the edge of the New Forest, the line passes under the A35 road bridge and runs along an embankment into Christchurch. Looking to the left it may be possible (on a clear day) to glimpse Hengistbury Head and the sea. Hengistbury Head forms a natural breakwater protecting a small natural harbour at Mudeford, formed in the lee from the prevailing south-westerly wind. A long sand spit has formed trailing off to the end of the Head. The initial formation of Hengistbury Head dates back approximately 60 million years.

Continuing west along the embankment we pass over Hawthorne Road Bridge, the scene of a severe landslip in February 1966, and over the River Mude and River Avon – perhaps the richest fishing river in the country, which is teeming with salmon. The railway now heads under Christchurch Road Bridge, sweeping around the curved platforms at Christchurch. To the left of the bridge is the site of a very tall signal box, which had to be elevated above the bridge level for the signalman to have a view of approaching trains. This signal box also controlled a goods yard and the former branch line to Hurn and Ringwood. On the left-hand side of the train it is possible to pick out the tower of Christchurch Priory, which is said to have the finest medieval interior in the country. The speed restriction through Christchurch Station was very frustrating to drivers of steam locomotives, as it prevented them from opening up to charge the 1½-mile 1 in 99 gradient towards Pokesdown. Before entering Pokesdown Station the line crosses over the 64-mile-long River Stour, which originates in Wiltshire and passes through Dorset before heading out into the estuary at Mudeford. Pokesdown Station was an important station with full-length platforms until the end of steam services in 1967. The station was provided with through lines for non-stop trains and had a track layout of four lines with an all-metal construction signal box. Since electrification this has now been rationalised. The next station on the line at Boscombe was closed on 4 October 1965 to passenger traffic, but the freight yard lingered on for a few years after. Today the station yard is occupied by a small industrial estate, but there have been proposals to reopen the station in the future. Trains now begin to slow as the line approaches Bournemouth.

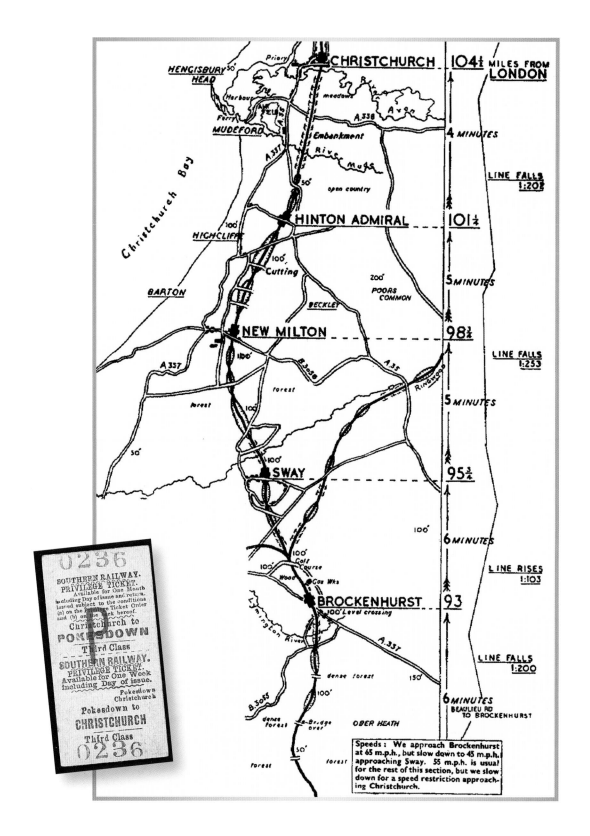

The blue and grey carriages indicate that there are just a few weeks to go before the end of steam. Rebuilt West Country Class No. 34021 *Dartmoor* approaches Lymington Junction with a down express to Bournemouth and Weymouth on 3 June 1967. (David Peters)

A rare and unexpected sight at Widden Bottom Bridge on Setley Plain on 19 June 1965 as ex-Eastleigh Works Midland Region Ivatt 2-6-0 No. 43088 is seen hauling the down 12.55 p.m. Eastleigh to Bournemouth stopping train as a running-in turn. The paintwork is immaculate and the boiler is steaming well, but the driver shouts out, 'She's very tight! Give me a Standard any day.' (Britton Collection)

BR Standard Class 5 No. 73002 leisurely creeps under Widden Bottom Bridge into Sway Cutting with a down stopping train to Bournemouth Central on 31 March 1967. (David Peters)

Maunsell S15 Class 4-6-0 No. 30839 bustles along under Sway Station bridge in August 1964 with the 5.50 p.m. Southampton Terminus to Bournemouth West train. (Britton Collection)

With steam to spare, rebuilt West Country Class No. 34098 *Templecombe* glides into Sway Station on 26 June 1965 with a Bournemouth–Waterloo up express. (David Peters)

BR Standard Class 4 4-6-0 No. 75076 pauses at Hinton Admiral Station on 19 June 1967 with an up Bournemouth Central to Eastleigh three-coach stopping train. (Bryan Hicks)

The station running-in board proclaims 'Christchurch for Southbourne-on-Sea'. Double-chimney BR Standard Class 4 No. 75074 restarts a down stopping train to Bournemouth Central in early 1967. (Britton Collection)

This historic view shows the very last up weekday steam-hauled stopping train calling at Pokesdown – the 5.42 p.m. Bournemouth Central to Eastleigh three-coach train on 7 July 1967, hauled by rebuilt West Country Class No. 34021 *Dartmoor*. (Britton Collection)

SOUTHERN RAILWAY.
Issued subject to the Bye-laws, Regulations & Conditions in the Company's Bills and Notices. Available on DAY of issue ONLY.
Pokesdown to
NEW MILTON
THIRD CLASS
Issued in exchange for Return ticket Issued by the Hants & Dorset Motor Services Ltd. upon payment of the supplementary charge of 1d.
NOT TRANSFERABLE.
2419

2nd - SINGLE   SINGLE - 2nd
Pokesdown to
Pokesdown Christchurch   Pokesdown Christchurch
CHRISTCHURCH
(S)   4d. Fare 4d.   (S)
For conditions see over For conditions see over
1524

15

BOURNEMOUTH

As the train bursts out from the short tunnel underneath Holdenhurst Road into Bournemouth Central railway station, 108 miles from Waterloo, the passenger has the feeling of entering a cathedral. Opened as Bournemouth East in 1885, it was renamed Bournemouth Central in 1899 until 10 July 1967, when the new electric era commenced.

The station was designed to resemble a winter garden and was the most impressive overall roofed station west of Waterloo. The station buildings are built with a fine brick with a second storey wall with airy windows, complete with an impressive 350ft long by 100ft wide glass canopy elevated 40ft above with glazed ends. In steam days the station had two through roads with a bay platform on the up side platform at the Southampton end, and a parcels bay at the Weymouth end. The down platform is the second longest in the country. To complete the scene there was a four-road locomotive depot, coaling yard and 65ft turntable at the western end of the up side of the station. Today this area is the site of a car park and little trace remains of the shed.

The scene at the Weymouth end of the station has substantially changed in recent years with the construction of the Wessex Way Flyover bridge.

Bournemouth Central Station was not provided with much in the way of carriage berthing sidings, as this was dealt with at Bournemouth West Station, where trains terminated. On occasion the centre through rails were used for short spells, but they were required for passing goods trains and the through Weymouth–Waterloo *Channel Islands Boat Express* trains.

Although the attractions of Bournemouth cannot be seen from the train, the town is well worth a visit. Historically, Bournemouth was part of Hampshire but under the 1974 local government reorganisation it joined Dorset. The location on the south coast of England with its warm welcoming sands made Bournemouth a popular destination for tourists travelling by rail. With the arrival of the railway, the town began to expand and develop, increasing in population from 17,000 to 60,000 by 1900. Today the population is approximately 183,500 and the town boasts a university. Bournemouth became popular in post-war Britain and the writer J.R.R. Tolkien regularly travelled down by train over a thirty-year period, staying in the same room at the Hotel Miramar, with a second room to write in. The comedian and actor Tony Hancock lived in Bournemouth and his father ran the

Railway Hotel on Holdenhurst Road. Hollywood actor Stewart Granger resided in Bournemouth and was a regular traveller to Waterloo from Bournemouth Central in steam days. One of the first visitors to Bournemouth Central Station was Robert Louis Stevenson, the author of *The Strange Case of Dr Jekyll and Mr Hyde* and *Kidnapped*. He lived locally at his house 'Skerryvore' on the west cliff, now called Alum Chine Road.

Besides the Waterloo–Weymouth line, Bournemouth is the home of three funicular railways: the East Cliff Railway, West Cliff Railway and Fisherman's Walk Cliff Railway. These popular Victorian railways are now owned by Bournemouth Borough Council and serve to link the seaside promenade with the cliff top at various points along the seafront.

The view from Holdenhurst Road Bridge of rebuilt Merchant Navy Class No. 35003 *Royal Mail* departing eastwards from Bournemouth Central Station with *Pines Express* on 9 September 1965. (Britton Collection)

A busy time on the up platform at Bournemouth Central Station on 20 June 1967 as Nine Elms Shed fireman Norman Prior tops up the 4,500-gallon tender tank with water, assisted by driver Gordon Porter. Once this job is done Prior will quickly push the 5-ton coal supply forward, ready for the return journey to Waterloo. The new coloured light signal is showing green, so every second counts. (Bryan Hicks)

BR Class 9F 2-10-0 has just arrived at Bournemouth Central with the Warwickshire Railway Society 'Somerset & Dorset Joint and Eastleigh Rail Tour' on 12 June 1965. According to passenger Michael Jakeman of Warwick, the climb up over the Mendips from Bath Green Park was shrouded in mist and damp weather. He added that the 9F did not perform well and at times the 2-10-0 was crawling at snail's pace! The 9F was replaced by the sprightlier West Country Class No. 34097 *Holsworthy* for the run down through the New Forest to Eastleigh. (Britton Collection)

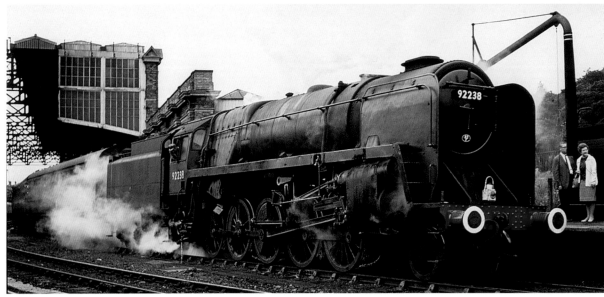

The smiling driver and his fireman standing just behind S15 No. 30838 peer out from the cab as they enter Bournemouth Central on 10 June 1963 with a pigeon special. (Bryan Hicks)

Drummond M7 tank slowly backs down onto the turntable at Bournemouth on 27 June 1962. (Britton Collection)

Sunlight penetrates the long dark shadows cast by the pine trees of Meryrick Park just west of Bournemouth Central Station to reveal rebuilt Merchant Navy Class No. 35003 *Royal Mail* with the up *Pines Express* on 9 September 1965. (Bryan Hicks)

Following the closure of Bournemouth West Station, trains using the carriage sidings had to access them via Branksome Station. Here BR Standard Class 5 No. 73119 *Elaine* sets back with empty carriage stock into the down platform at Branksome on 20 August 1966. Note the running-in board on the platform, which states 'Branksome for Canford Cliffs'. (Britton Collection)

The no preserved rebuilt Merchant Navy Class No. 35028 Clan Line rests at the buffer stops at Bournemouth West station on 4 August 1962, shortly after arriving from Waterloo. (Britton Collection)

By Train to
BOURNEMOUTH

Bournemouth is reached from London (Waterloo) in two hours (or just over) by a frequent service of restaurant car expresses and also by through trains from the West, Midlands and the North.

BOURNEMOUTH
The Most Favoured Resort

The "Bournemouth Belle" runs every day in each direction between London (Waterloo) and Bournemouth. The train is made up entirely of Pullman Cars, and the supplementary fees for the single journey are 1st class 6/-, 2nd class 4/-.

Specimen Ordinary Return fares to
BOURNEMOUTH from:

		2nd Class	1st Class
London (Waterloo)	(C)	36/-	54/-
Birmingham	(C)	56/-	84/-
Bristol	(C)	35/4	53/-
Cardiff	(C)	47/8	71/6
Edinburgh	(C)	167/-	250/6
Exeter-Central	(W)	31/8	47/6
Glasgow	(C)	170/-	255/-
Liverpool	(W)	84/4	126/6
Manchester	(W)	82/4	123/6
Sheffield	(C)	76/8	115/-
York	(C)	92/-	138/-

(C) To Bournemouth Central.   (W) To Bournemouth West.

★ **MID-WEEK HOLIDAY RETURN TICKETS** to Bournemouth are obtainable at many stations during the Summer at reduced fares.

★ **"THE PINES EXPRESS."**—Through train to Bournemouth every weekday from Manchester, Stockport, Liverpool, Crewe, Birmingham, etc.

★ **THROUGH TRAINS** also during the Summer from Swansea, Cardiff, Newport, Bristol, Bath Spa, Birkenhead, Chester, Shrewsbury, Wolverhampton, Birmingham, Newcastle, Durham, Darlington, Sunderland, West Hartlepool, Stockton, York, Bradford, Leeds, Huddersfield, Sheffield, Derby, Nottingham, Leicester, Rugby, etc. Through services are also available from many of these places during the Winter months.

★ **HOLIDAY RUNABOUT TICKETS.**—During the Summer months see the district cheaply with a Runabout ticket.

★ **CHEAP DAY TICKETS** are issued daily from Bournemouth to surrounding places of interest.

For further details and any information regarding train services including through trains, fares, seat reservations, runabout tickets, luggage in advance, etc., enquire at Stations, Offices, and principal Travel Agencies.

BRITISH RAILWAYS

Bournemouth photographs by John T. Etches, Bournemouth

D. R. HILLMAN LTD., FROME   PRINTED IN ENGLAND

16

BOURNEMOUTH TO WAREHAM

After leaving Bournemouth the railway enters a cutting passing Meyrick Park and descends into the upper Bourne Valley. Meyrick Park, three-quarters of a mile from Bournemouth Central, had its own station opened on 1 March 1906, but it closed as a wartime economy on 1 November 1917.

At Gasworks Junction there used to be a triangular junction for Bournemouth West Station, which officially closed on 4 October 1965. This station was terminus for most through services from Waterloo and the terminus for trains from Salisbury, Brockenhurst via Ringwood and the 'Old Road' line and Bath on the Somerset & Dorset line. Bournemouth West was the destination for such legendary trains as the *Bournemouth Belle* Pullman train and the *Pines Express*.

Although passenger services were withdrawn at Bournemouth West Station on a temporary basis for completion of electrification, on 6 September 1965 it became permanent. 'Ghost trains' continued to start and terminate from the disused platforms at Bournemouth West up to the end of steam in 1967. With the completion of electrification the station was demolished to make way for the A338 Wessex Way road. However, a new Train Care depot was constructed on the site of the former carriage sidings.

After crossing the Bourne Valley Viaduct the next feature on the main line from Bournemouth to Weymouth is Branksome Station, which retains the western connection to Bournemouth West. The LSWR opened the Southampton to Weymouth line in January 1857, but the station at Branksome was not opened until 1893. The booking hall was elevated above the platforms at road level with a covered footbridge. The Somerset & Dorset Railway opened a small locomotive depot at Branksome in 1895, which operated until closure of the line to Bournemouth West in 1965. This was the working base for S&D footplate crews of the *Pines Express* such as driver Donald Beale and fireman Peter Smith, driver Johnny Walker and fireman Aubrey Punter. Cockney Nine Elms Shed footplate crews would visit Branksome Shed daily while their locomotives were being serviced. This would lead to great rivalry when comparing locomotives and routes while playing inter-shed card games.

From Branksome the line descends steeply at 1 in 60 down the notorious Parkstone Bank and through Parkstone Station to Poole. Just beyond Parkstone Station on the left-hand side is an embankment and the former railway-owned land. This was where the sludge trains from Bournemouth Shed water purification plant would deposit lime deposits once a fortnight. It was also the dumping ground for locomotive ash and oil waste from the steam locomotives. Today this site boasts luxury penthouse apartments, which command some of the highest real estate prices in the area!

Parkstone Bank was a notoriously challenging obstacle for footplate crews in steam days for up trains, since they could not charge the bank at Poole owing to severe speed restrictions on the curve. Consequently, trains climbing the gradient up out of Poole would be required to take an assisting banking locomotive at the rear of the train. The running-in board at Parkstone Station referred to 'Parkstone for Sandbanks'. Sandbanks is a nearby dormitory area overlooking Poole Harbour and Brownsea Island with the chain ferry connection to Studland and the Isle of Purbeck. This can be viewed on the left of the train as it descends the elevated curving causeway into Poole.

The approach into Poole was quite impressive in steam days as the line curved sharply and crossed over the gated level crossings at High Street and Towngate Street. Today a flyover road has changed the landscape and now traffic movements are much clearer. An 1872-built footbridge (provided for shoppers to cross the line) was an ideal vantage point to observe trains entering and departing from Poole. The original station buildings were situated on the up platform at Poole, but the local structure redevelopment plan in the late 1980s swept them away and the station was repositioned to the west and the road flyover was constructed. Up until May 1960 there was a goods line to Poole Quay, which joined the main line at the Weymouth end of the station. The line ran along part of what is now the Holes Bay relief road and down West Quay Road. Former LSWR 0-4-0 B4 Class tank engines could be seen hauling transfer loads in wagons to local paddle steamers and coasters.

Poole can trace its routes back to the Iron Age. The Romans landed at Poole during the first century. In Anglo-Saxon times Poole was part of the Kingdom of Wessex and began to develop as a port. Poole experienced two large-scale Viking attacks when Guthrum sailed his fleet of longships through the harbour to attack Wareham in AD 876 and later, when Canute began his conquest of England in 1015. Following the Norman Conquest, Poole rapidly grew into a busy port. This was recognised by King Henry VI in 1433 with the award of staple port status, allowing the export of wool and the construction of a town wall. During the English Civil War the town of Poole sided with Cromwell's Parliamentarians and escaped attack from the Royalists in 1646.

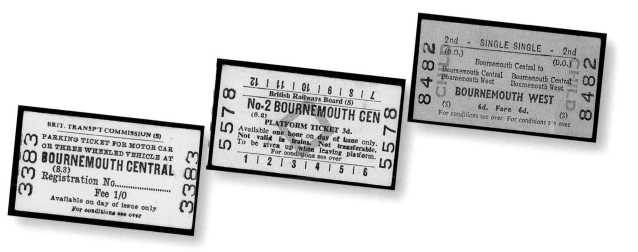

During the Second World War Poole was the third largest embarkation point for the D-Day Operation Overload Normandy landings. Eighty-one landing craft containing troops from the United States 29th Infantry Division and the US Army Rangers departed for Omaha Beach. In 1954 the Royal Marines established a home at Hamworthy to the 1st Assault Group Royal Marines and Special Boat Service. Passengers from passing trains can often spot marines and commandos in training.

Poole is also the headquarters of the Royal National Lifeboat Institute and new lifeboats can be seen on their trials in Poole Harbour.

The harbour is the largest natural harbour in Europe and lays claim to the title of the second largest natural harbour in the world after Sydney Harbour in Australia. Poole Harbour contains several small islands that can be viewed from the carriage window of the train. The largest island is Brownsea Island, which is owned by the National Trust. Brownsea is the birthplace of Lord Baden Powell's Scout movement. Huge oil and natural gas reserves extend under Poole Harbour and Britain's largest onshore oil field operates from Wytch Farm.

About half a mile north-west from Poole Station the line curves to cross Holes Bay and the views from the train are quite breathtaking. Beyond is Hamworthy Junction Station, which opened as Poole Junction in 1847. Until 1964 through trains to Weymouth using the 'Old Road' via Ringwood to avoid Bournemouth would join the main line at Hamworthy. Similarly, trains coming off the Somerset & Dorset line from Bath to Swanage and Weymouth would use this connection. A small motive power depot and coal stage built by the LSWR in 1847 remained in use until 3 May 1954 at Hamworthy. The track work, however, remained in use until 1975. Hamworthy is also the junction where a freight branch to Hamworthy Goods and Quay runs from. This was a busy freight branch in steam days and was the home of the industrial 0-4-0 tank engines *Bonnie Prince Charlie* (now preserved at Didcot Railway Centre) and sister engine *Western Pride*.

The line remains level to the next station at Holton Heath, but halfway between Hamworthy and Holton Heath the line crosses Lytchett Bay and Wareham Channel across a beautiful two-bow string-span cast-iron bridge. Holton Heath Station was opened to serve the Royal Navy Cordite Factory during the First World War and did not open to the public until 14 July 1924. To model railway enthusiasts, the name Holton Heath is synonymous with the original home of Graham Farish (Grafar) Models N and OO gauge scale trains, now part of Bachmann Europe.

The line now passes through Westfield Copse before entering Wareham Station. The current station was opened in 1887 and replaced the original opened in 1847. The crossing at the east end of the station next to the signal box was originally the main road level crossing and a notorious bottleneck for traffic. The station had two bay platforms that served the Swanage branch from 1885 until closure in 1972. There are realistic imminent plans to reopen the branch to Swanage for regular train services from the junction at Worgret to Corfe Castle and Swanage.

Leaving Wareham on the left-hand side, the walls of Wareham can be discerned through the window. As the train heads across Wareham Common it passes over the River Piddle, which frequently bursts its banks during the winter months. Approaching Worgret Junction the line passes under the bridge carrying the Wareham to Wool A352 road.

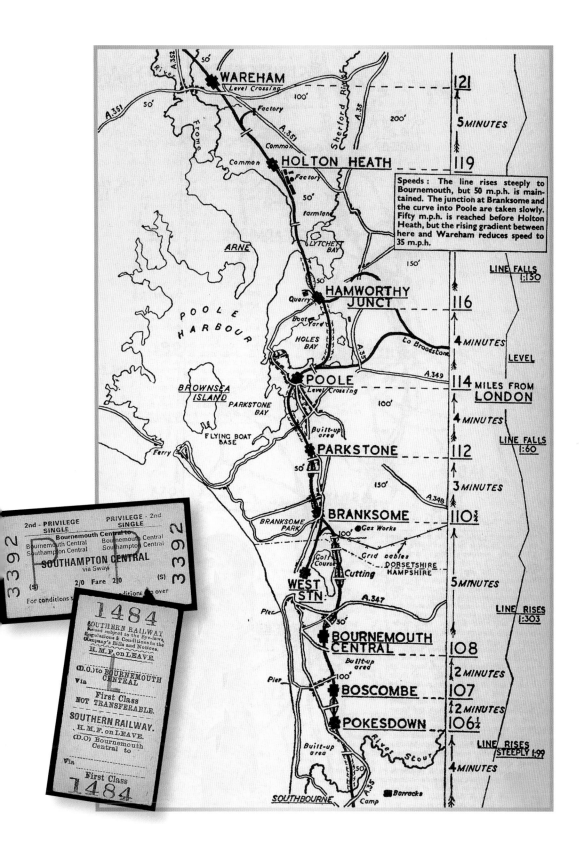

BR Standard Class 5 No. 73037, hauling a featherweight train stopping service from Weymouth, is perfectly framed in one of the three arches of the attractive overbridge spanning the cutting near the summit of Parkstone Bank as she storms up the 1 in 60 gradient on 21 June 1967. (Bryan Hicks)

BR Standard Class 5 No. 76027 is toiling up the 1 in 60 gradient of Parkstone Bank with an up three-coach local stopping train from Weymouth on 19 September 1965. (Bryan Hicks)

Whitecliff Road Bridge, with Parkstone Bay on the left and Poole Park Boating Lake on the right. Two local children and their mother peer up to watch rebuilt Merchant Navy Class No. 35013 *Blue Funnel* drift down the gradient and across the curved embankment into Poole on 21 June 1967. (Bryan Hicks)

BR Standard Class 4 No. 76006 on the six-coach 12.12 p.m. train from Weymouth attacks the climb out of Poole at Whitecliff Road Bridge on 20 June 1966. In the foreground is Parkstone Bay and Whitecliff Park. (Britton Collection)

The gates of Towngate Street level crossing are open to vehicles and pedestrians, as rebuilt Merchant Navy 35030 *Elder Dempster Lines* on the 12.51 p.m service waits at Poole Station on 13 July 1966. (Britton Collection)

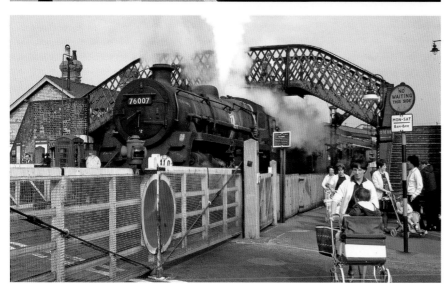

Prams and pushchairs at Poole Station on 27 August 1966. The gates are closed to allow BR Standard Class 4 No. 76007 to start away from Poole Station with an up local train from Weymouth. (Britton Collection)

Photographer David Peters
has captured this scene at
Holes Bay to perfection:
rebuilt Bulleid Pacific
No. 34071 *601 Squadron*
coasts around the curve on
the causeway embankment
from Hamworthy Junction
with an up Weymouth–
Waterloo express on 26 June
1965. (David Peters)

A rarely photographed scene of
steam on Hamworthy Quay as the
preserved *Bonnie Prince Charlie*
undertakes duties shunting coal
wagons. (Britton Collection)

With just days to go before the
end of steam on the Southern, BR
Standard 5 No. 73093 departs from
Wareham to Weymouth on 1 July
1967. (Britton Collection)

17

WORGRET JUNCTION TO MORETON

Having passed Worgret Junction, we continue our journey westward. In steam days, this section of line was a noted racing ground, where trains would travel at some speed. We pass Holme Lane Crossing, which spans the River Frome. Here a small party of Cavaliers held the bridge against Oliver Cromwell's Roundheads. Heading along the straight we pass East Stoke Crossing with the church on our right. Approaching Wool on the left are the ruins of Bindon Abbey and on the opposite side the Woolbridge Manor House, a fourteenth-century building. It is associated with Thomas Hardy's classic 1892 novel *Tess of the d'Urbervilles*.

In steam days Wool was a very busy station and passengers alighted here for the nearby Lulworth Cove and Durdle Door. The original name board, which lasted until the rebuilding of the station, proclaimed 'Wool for Lulworth Cove'. The station opened on 1 June 1847 as part of the Southampton & Dorchester Railway, but was amalgamated into the London South Western Railway the following year. In 1906, Frederick Treves wrote, 'Wool was once a pretty village, but the railway has contaminated it.' One can only wonder what he would have thought about the effect of the motor car!

It was also a major interchange point for troops heading for Bovington Camp. The name Wool is of interest as it derives from the word 'spring' and to this day a stream runs through the village. Today the great attractions on the doorstep are Monkey World, the Tank Museum and Cloud's Hill, the former home of T.E. Lawrence 'of Arabia'. At one time there was a military railway from Wool to Bovington Camp, which closed on 4 November 1928.

During the early part of the Second World War two aircraft returning from a raid on Portland naval base began to circle Wool Station, having spotted smoke and steam from two engines shunting in the station yard. A Drummond T9 locomotive from Dorchester, which was shunting next to the Ship Inn, was strafed, but no lives were lost in the raid. In post-war years two redundant Pullman carriages, Cars 15 and 30, were placed on the up side of the line and converted into 'holiday coaches'.

Heading away over the crossing at Wool, which has long been a bottleneck for through traffic, the train skirts the site of one of Britain's pioneer atomic power plants on the left at Winfrith. The Dorset landscape now changes to one of heathland, the habitat of rare sand lizards, slow worms and adders. Approaching Moreton on the left are great sand pits, providing vast supplies of building sand to the construction industry. The First World War hero Lawrence of Arabia is buried in Moreton churchyard, while the heart of the author Thomas Hardy is enshrined in the church of Stinsford, a village seen on the right of the railway.

Unlike Wool, Moreton is over a mile away from its station, which is situated on the south bank of the River Frome. Moreton Station boasted crossing gates, a cattle dock and sidings leading to a gravel yard and brickyard, controlled by a delightful LSWR-style signal box, which closed on 16 February 1972. The main buildings were on the up platform, the reverse of the arrangement at Wool.

During the 1950s, the Lord Nelson Class No. 30854 *Howard of Effingham* had the misfortune to get its whistle stuck open all the way from Moreton Station to Wareham. By Wareham the driver of the up express had come to the end of his patience and climbed out onto the running plate with a monkey wrench to rectify the noisy problem!

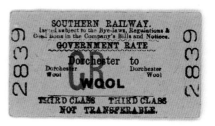

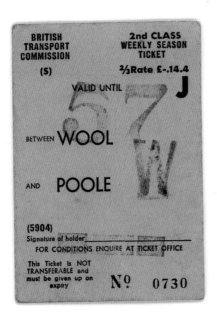

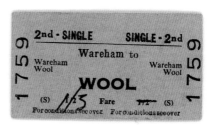

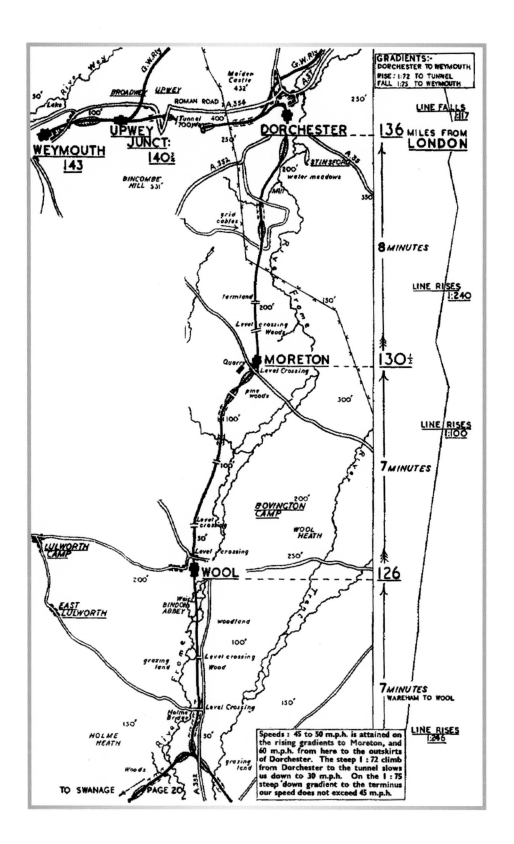

Speeds : 45 to 50 m.p.h. is attained on the rising gradients to Moreton, and 60 m.p.h. from here to the outskirts of Dorchester. The steep 1 : 72 climb from Dorchester to the tunnel slows us down to 30 m.p.h. On the 1 : 75 steep down gradient to the terminus our speed does not exceed 45 m.p.h.

Approaching Holme Crossing at speed on 18 June 1967 is the RCTS 'Farewell To Southern Steam Rail Tour', hauled by rebuilt Bulleid Light Pacific No. 34089 *602 Squadron* and bound for Weymouth. (Britton Collection)

Threatening clouds greet BR Standard 4 No. 76059, which is hauling a down Bournemouth Central–Weymouth stopper, at East Stoke Crossing on 8 August 1966. (Britton Collection)

Wool Station, complete with luggage trolleys and typical Southern platform furniture. (Britton Collection)

BR Standard Class 4 No. 76031, with an up four-coach Weymouth-Eastleigh stopper, clanks her way under Broomhill Bridge, Winfrith, on 3 June 1967. (Britton Collection)

The filthy-looking rebuilt Merchant Navy Class No. 35030 *Elder Dempster Line*, hauling the up 1.25 p.m. Weymouth–Waterloo, roars through east of Wool heading towards Wareham on 8 August 1966. (Britton Collection)

Salisbury Shed's rebuilt West Country Class No. 34013 *Okehampton* is in full flight, heading past Westwood on Winfrith Heath near Moreton with a down express for Weymouth. (Britton Collection)

18

MORETON TO DORCHESTER

The line from Moreton passes the site of RAF Warmwell at Crossways on the left-hand side of the train. In the early 1930s the Air Ministry acquired the heath and farmland to build an airfield, which was completed in 1937. The airfield was to become a major fighter base during the Battle of Britain, offering fighter protection for the nearby Portland Naval Base and Devonport. Today the runways have almost disappeared as a result of sand and gravel extraction. As the railway runs into Dorchester it passes over a series of crossings at Woodsford and West Stafford.

Dorchester has two stations: Dorchester South on the Waterloo–Weymouth line and Dorchester West on the Bristol–Yeovil–Weymouth line. The track layout of Dorchester South was probably unique in the British Isles. It was built as an east-end-facing terminus with the intention of continuing the line west towards Exeter and Plymouth. These plans were never realised and instead another line was built to link up with the Great Western line to Weymouth and a new down platform on the curve was built. Dorchester South Station up platform remained a terminus platform and Weymouth–Bournemouth trains had to pass the station and then reverse into it, before continuing their journey. This time-consuming procedure continued until 1970, three years after the end of steam when a new up platform was built on the curve.

Until 1957 Dorchester South had its own motive power depot with a coal stage and turntable. The shed was at the south side of the station. The shed's major duties were passenger trains between Weymouth and Bournemouth, but before the First World War Dorchester locos and crews worked through trains to Waterloo via the 'Old Road' and Ringwood. The allocation of locomotives rarely exceeded twenty engines, but the pride of the shed was Drummond T9 No. 30119, which was the 'Royal Engine' and reserved for hauling the Royal Train in polished Southern green livery. In 1938 some of the Lord Nelson Class engines were fitted with speed recorders and it was Dorchester crews who managed to exceed 'the ton' on up expresses through Wool! An unusual feature of Dorchester loco shed was the method of access to and from the running lines as engines entered the shed directly from the down main line. A set of points actually operated from inside the shed under the control of the station signal box. This was something of an inconvenience and meant that, effectively, Dorchester Shed only possessed three roads instead of the four. With the closure of the

Southern branch line from Weymouth to Portland in 1952, Dorchester Shed declined with reduced duties and became a sub-shed of Bournemouth until closure in 1957.

The original signal box, which lasted up until September 1959, was unusually tall to allow the signalman complete visual coverage of the station, its approaches, freight sidings and the locomotive shed. The signal lever frame was unusual in that it was at right angles to the tracks. On windy days a south-westerly wind would whistle through the glass window panes and the steps could be very slippery on damp autumnal days and with ice in the winter months.

Just opposite the station are Dorchester Market and the former Eldridge Pope Brewery. Dorchester Brewery opened in 1879 with its own water supply and access to the railway, which meant that its fine beers and traditional ales in wooden barrels could easily be transported from London to Exeter. The company became the wine supplier to Queen Victoria and was one of the first to be awarded the Royal Warrant.

Dorchester is the county town of Dorset and is an historic market town lying on the banks of the River Frome. The town is noted for being the home and inspiration of the author Thomas Hardy, whose novel *The Mayor of Casterbridge* was based on the town. Dorchester can trace its roots back to pre-historic times.

In the first century the Romans garrisoned Dorchester, naming it Durnovaria. The settlement was walled by the Romans and remains of this can still be seen today. As the train heads away from Dorchester South, passengers may wish to cast their eyes to the right to see Maumury Rings. This is a Neolithic henge, a large circular earthwork with a single bank and ditch. In the first century, the site was converted into a Roman amphitheatre. During the English Civil War the site was reused as an artillery position for guarding the southern approach to Dorchester.

Dorchester is also known for the trial of the Tolpuddle Martyrs at the Shire Hall Court in 1833. This building remains and is preserved as it was at the time. The Trade Union Movement can trace its origins back to the Tolpuddle Martyrs, who were arrested for forming the Friendly Society of Agricultural Labourers and swearing an oath of allegiance.

An unidentified rebuilt Bulleid Pacific, heading a down express for Weymouth, clatters through Moreton Station at speed. On the left of the picture is the signal box that controlled the crossing gates until they were replaced by automatic barriers. (Britton Collection)

Rebuilt Merchant Navy Class No. 35023 *Holland Africa Line*, hauling an up stopping train, slows as she draws in to Moreton Station. (Britton Collection)

West Country Class No. 34019 *Bideford* races towards Weymouth with the Warwickshire Railway Society special to Weymouth on 5 September 1965. She is pictured at West Stafford crossing near Frome Farm, just east of Dorchester. The village of West Stafford can be seen on the left of the train, with Parsonage Plantation and Sandy Barrow Ridge on the right. (Bryan Hicks)

No. 34087 *145 Squadron* makes a smoky departure with an up train from Dorchester South on 4 February 1967. (Martin Robinson Collection)

Packed with sad railway enthusiasts eager to be part of the final hours of Southern Steam, rebuilt Merchant Navy Class No. 35003 *Royal Mail* starts away from Dorchester South Station bound for Weymouth, hauling the 8.35 a.m. Waterloo–Weymouth on 7 July 1967, working her penultimate down train. (Britton Collection)

Stopping at Dorchester South Station for the final time whilst hauling the 9.00 p.m. Bournemouth–Weymouth train is rebuilt Merchant Navy No. 35003 *Royal Mail*. (Britton Collection)

On board the 9.00 p.m. Bournemouth–Weymouth train on 7 July 1967, behind rebuilt Merchant Navy No. 35003 *Royal Mail* departing from Dorchester South for the very last time. On arrival at Weymouth, No. 35003 will run light up to the shed, drop the fire and be withdrawn from service for scrapping. (Britton Collection)

Rebuilt Bulleid Pacific No. 34037 *Clovelly* rounds the sharp curve at Dorchester South from Weymouth with the last steam-hauled up *Channel Islands Boat Express* on 7 July 1967. (Britton Collection)

19

DORCHESTER JUNCTION TO WEYMOUTH

The sharply curving line from Dorchester South joins the former Great Western line from Yeovil and Dorchester West at Dorchester Junction. Passengers can glimpse the remains of the ancient Iron Age hill fort of Maiden Castle, which can be seen from the train on the right-hand side after leaving Dorchester. Maiden Castle was one of the most powerful settlements in pre-Roman Britain with tribes having existed there since 4000 BC. The Romans defeated the local tribes by AD 70 and there is evidence of a massacre at Maiden Castle.

The line now begins to descend towards Weymouth through two short tunnels and past the former Upwey Wishing Well Halt and through Upwey Junction Station, which was the start of the former GWR branch to Abbotsbury, closed in 1952.

In steam days one of the most enduring images was of almost every train over eight coaches requiring banking assistance up Bincombe Bank (also known as Upwey Bank) out of Weymouth. It was famed as one of the most fearsome climbs in Southern England. Starting out from Weymouth it was quite easy going to Radipole, which was just over a mile from the terminus. From here, however, the line angles steeply upward on a slope of 1 in 74 for a mile and a third. The gradient increases to 1 in 50 beyond Upwey Junction. Western Region trains always received banking assistance at the rear of the train, as far as the north end of the 814yd Bincombe Tunnel. A crossover and refuge siding between the up and down lines were provided for banking engines opposite the Bincombe signal box. The Southern Region trains took on a pilot at the front to double head as far as Dorchester South Station. Former Weymouth driver Eddie Prangnell had a harrowing experience in Bincombe Tunnel when driving an un-rebuilt West Country with just four coaches: 'It was a damp morning and I felt confident I would be ok with just four coaches climbing out of Weymouth. How wrong I was. After losing our feet in the tunnel, we eventually arrived at Dorchester South 20 minutes late!'

By the early 1960s Weymouth engines covered the banking turns for both Western and Southern Region routes. In July and August 1963, two 80xxx BR Standard 4MTs were sent to Weymouth to assist with banking duties. At the end of August 1963 they were replaced by Ivatt 2-6-2 tanks. Over the final years of steam, however, in practice banking and piloting duties were performed by any spare engine including: BR Standard 4MTs and 5MTs, Bulleid Light Pacifics and Merchant Navy Pacifics. The favourite place to picnic, photograph and watch the steam engines barking up the bank was at Upwey Wishing Well Halt just south of the tunnel entrance. Here one had a wonderful panoramic view overlooking Weymouth Bay and Portland. The progress of trains ascending the bank could be followed all the way up from Weymouth through Radipole Halt, past Upwey Junction Station and up the testing climb. If the wind was blowing in the right direction, it was possible to hear the cock-crow whistles as the train announced its departure from Weymouth. George III drank from the wishing well at Upwey, using a gold cup that is still presented annually at Ascot Races.

Historically, Weymouth was a GWR town and the shed was located three-quarters of a mile from the terminus station. It was coded 82F by British Railways Western Region, but in February 1958 it became part of the Southern Region of British Railways and was recoded 71G and later 70G after September 1963. The 175ft x 50ft brick-built shed was a standard straight road GWR design building with a repair shop partially roofed by a water tank. At the rear of the shed was a lifting hoist for locomotive repairs. Adjacent to this was a 65ft GWR-style turntable and a 30ft x 32ft coal stage. The lack of local labour in the 1960s resulted in a Massey Ferguson tractor equipped with a shovel being hired periodically to clear the yard of ash debris and coal.

In the 1950s the Western Region had responsibility for Weymouth and regular services went to Bristol Temple Meads, via Bath, Bradford Upon Avon and Westbury. The main route to London in those days was to Paddington from Weymouth and this lasted until the end of 1960. The Western Region passenger services from Weymouth to Paddington ran via Westbury, Newbury and Reading and took about four hours. A regular through service during the summer was the Wolverhampton–Weymouth train, via Leamington Spa, Oxford and Swindon. Observations at Leamington Spa confirm that it was a lightly loaded train, except for the 'Coventry holiday fortnight', and often pulled by a Hall Class engine. The highlight on Western services at Weymouth during the summer timetable, until November 1959, was the *Channel Islands Boat Express* to Paddington, which was normally hauled by an Old Oak Common Castle Class. During the summer season freight traffic over the Western route was intensive, with up to seven perishable trains mostly carrying tomatoes. They were mainly hauled by 28xx 2-8-0s, 43xx 2-6-0s or Halls. However, in the final years of steam operation, these perishable freight trains were hauled by BR Standard 5MTs and even SR Bulleid West Country Class Pacifics! Local service trains to Yeovil Pen Mill, via Dorchester West, and Maiden Newton were generally hauled by 14xx 0-4-2 tanks and 45xx 2-6-2 tanks. Steam began rapidly to decline on Western Region local services and through trains owing to dieselisation from the summer of 1959.

Perhaps the most unusual aspect of railway operation in Weymouth was the Weymouth Quay line or 'The Tramway' as it was popularly known. Every visiting tourist knew about it as trains would stop the traffic and quite often trains would be held up by parked cars. It was a tramway line from Weymouth Junction to the Quay, where trains connected with the boats to the Channel Islands. Small 1366 0-6-0 Pannier tanks were the normal locomotives to handle operations, but 57xx Panniers and later Ivatt 2-6-2 tanks were not uncommon on the Quay until dieselisation.

By the late 1950s to early 1960s the Portland and Easton branch was closed to regular passenger services. Occasional troop trains hauled by 43xx and BR Standard 76xxx Class 2-6-0s and enthusiast specials ran down the branch until 27 March 1965, when Ivatt tanks 41324 and 41284 topped and tailed a six-coach train. The final freight working was on Friday 9 April 1965. The station at Melcombe

Regis was the first station on the branch and consisted of a single platform. When passenger services on the branch ceased in 1952, the station continued to see occasional use as a terminal facility for main-line trains on summer Saturdays. This relieved pressure on the main Weymouth station, which was almost opposite.

The perishable and parcels traffic arriving and departing from Weymouth was enormous in steam days. It was possible to see tomato trains working out via the Western Region line at Dorchester to Westbury right up to the final day of steam on 9 July 1967. During the summer season 'Passenger Luggage in Advance' traffic was a feature with tourists to the resort sending their cases ahead of them. Luggage was dispatched on Friday nights to local hotels and guest houses ready for arrivals the following day and the returning luggage was collected.

A regular feature at Weymouth Station in the 1960s was the berthing of the mail train. In the summer of 1962, this up passenger and postal train departed from Weymouth at 10.13 p.m., calling at Dorchester South, Wool, Wareham, Poole, Bournemouth Central, Christchurch, Brockenhurst and thence to Southampton Terminus and Waterloo. A corresponding down passenger and postal train departed from Waterloo at 10.35 p.m. The stock was always fascinating to inspect as it contained two green-liveried Maunsell-built Travelling Post Office sorting van plus one stowage van with the gold lettering 'Royal Mail' and a coat of arms embellishing the side panels. These special postal vans were fascinating with their offset corridor connections and a purpose-built letterbox provided in the side panelling. This set of vans was padded out with additional mail vans and two passenger carriages.

There were many special trains visiting Weymouth in steam days and a few stand out in the memory. On Wednesday 29 April 1959 Her Majesty The Queen visited the warships at Portland Dockyard. This brought the nine-coach Royal Train to Weymouth hauled by West Country class No. 34048 *Crediton*. This engine was polished to perfection with mirror finish silver buffers and rods to complement the shining paintwork. The West Country class engine was replaced at Weymouth by two Western Region Panniers Nos 3737 and 4689 to convey the Royal Train down the Portland branch and return. Weymouth shed cleaners had spent two days on each engine to ensure that every nut and bolt, coupling, the buffers and the paint work was spick and span. So proud of their achievement, the final touch was to whitewash the coal in the bunker for the occasion! For the return journey the gallant little Panniers were replaced by West Country Class No. 34048 *Crediton* and No. 34046 *Braunton*. At the entrance to Weymouth Shed the Foreman, shed staff and footplate crews stood in line to watch Her Majesty pass. It was a very proud moment for all.

The second special train that really comes to mind is the visit of former LNER Gresley Pacific No. 60024 *Kingfisher*, while hauling the A4 Locomotive Preservation Society 'Victory Railtour' on 26 March 1966. While visiting Weymouth Shed for turning and servicing, practically all the local footplate crews on duty came out to inspect this streamlined Pacific. The comments heard were quite amusing: 'Where do they put the key in to wind her up?' – 'I bet a Merchant or a Castle would lick her going up Upwey bank anyday!' On her return heading up Upwey bank, although banked at the rear by BR Standard Five No. 73114, the LNER racehorse showed just what she was made of. The message soon got back to Weymouth footplate crews who eagerly welcomed sister A4 *Sir Nigel Gresley* the following year.

The town of Weymouth can trace its history back to the twelfth century, when one of the most devastating pandemics in human history entered England, carried by oriental rat-fleas living on the black rats that were regular passengers on merchant ships entering Weymouth.

King Henry VIII had two Device Forts built to protect the Dorset coast from invasion in the 1530s at Sandsfoot in Wyke Regis and Portland Castle in Castletown. Sadly parts of Sandsfoot have crumbled and fallen into the sea due to coastal erosion. Portland Harbour's other famous fort is the Nothe Fort, which was built in 1872 to protect the harbour. The fort played an important part in the Second World War in preparation for D-Day by American forces. The fort was abandoned in 1956, but preserved by the local council in 1961. Today Nothe Fort is an outstanding museum featuring Second World War memorabilia, including scale models and preserved vehicles.

By the eighteenth century fewer people were employed in trading and local fishing and the town began to develop as a tourist resort. The introduction of the railways resulted in Weymouth becoming a cross-Channel ferry port to the Channel Islands and France. Express freight trains for many years carried fresh Channel Islands tomatoes and vegetables to London and the Midlands, via the Quay tramway. Today this trade has disappeared and Weymouth Harbour is filled with pleasure boats and private yachts. The nearby Portland Harbour, once an important Royal Navy base, is the home of the Weymouth & Portland National Sailing Academy. More recently the sailing events of the 2012 Olympic Games and Paralympic Games were held in Portland Harbour. Portland is well known for the Portland Bill Lighthouse and for Portland stone, which was used to build major public buildings including St Paul's Cathedral and Buckingham Palace in London. Portland stone was also exported to construct the United Nations Building in New York. At one time regular freight trains ran down the Portland branch railway from Easton to convey Portland stone to all parts of the country.

Many will remember Weymouth by the Osmington White Horse, a hill figure sculpted into the limestone just north of Weymouth. The horse's rider is King George III, who regularly visited Weymouth. The 280ft long by 323ft high landmark can be seen for miles around.

Weymouth was the home port of Cosens, best known for their paddle steamers, which from 1848 until 1967 took tourists on trips along the Jurassic Coast to Poole and Bournemouth, and on occasions to Cherbourg and the Channel Islands. Passengers on the paddle steamer the *Empress of India* would regularly be accompanied on cruises by two chimpanzees who would pose for souvenir photos. Today the preserved paddle steamer PS *Waverley* regularly calls at Weymouth Pier for summer cruises to Swanage, Poole, Bournemouth and around the Isle of Wight.

To many generations of families the greatest attraction of Weymouth is the golden sandy beaches, the donkeys, Punch & Judy and the sand sculptor. The nearby Radipole Lake has a magnetic appeal not only as an environmental conservation area but also as a venue to sail scale-model boats.

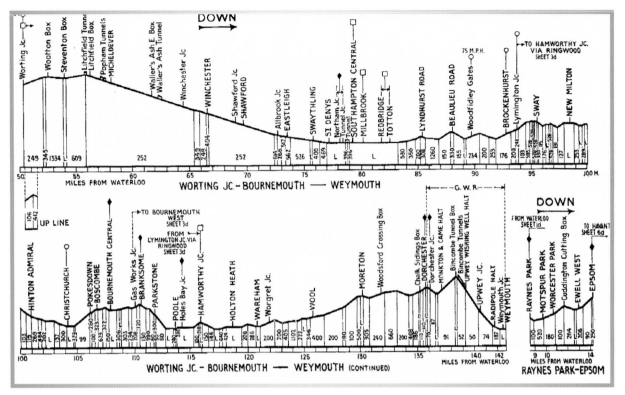

WORTING JC.—BOURNEMOUTH — WEYMOUTH

WORTING JC.—BOURNEMOUTH — WEYMOUTH (CONTINUED)

RAYNES PARK-EPSOM

Rebuilt Merchant Navy Class No. 35030 *Elder Dempster Lines* bursts out of Bincombe Tunnel with the 8.35 a.m. Waterloo–Weymouth on 15 June 1967. (David Peters)

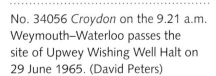

No. 34056 *Croydon* on the 9.21 a.m. Weymouth–Waterloo passes the site of Upwey Wishing Well Halt on 29 June 1965. (David Peters)

BR Standard Class 4 No. 80138 pilots rebuilt West Country Class No. 34024 *Tamar Valley*, hauling the 15.50 Weymouth–Waterloo up Upwey Bank on 11 June 1965. (Britton Collection)

Looking from the signal box at Upwey & Broadwey Station on 8 June 1967, we see un-rebuilt West Country Class No. 34102 *Lapford* hauling a van train, banked at the rear by BR Standard 4 2-6-0 No. 76007. (Britton Collection)

BR Standard 4 2-6-0 No. 76067 is nearing the end of her days in this picture taken in June 1967. The fireman is smiling to the driver as they are plotting to thrash their engine up after the stop at Upwey & Broadwey up the 1 in 50 Upwey Bank to Dorchester South. The noise from the exhaust bark of the single chimney will be almost deafening! The driver has only a few more turns before he too will be retiring. (Britton Collection)

Castle Class 4-6-0 No. 7003 *Elmley Castle* has just worked in to Weymouth with a featherweight two-coach stopping train from Yeovil on 16 May 1964. Having loaded up with coal and been turned, the lubricator boxes are now being topped up with oil by the driver. The GWR Castle, magnificent in its heyday, is now absolutely filthy, and it was humiliating to see this once proud engine on such mundane duties. (Britton Collection)

Ivatt 2 tank No. 41298 gingerly returns along Weymouth Quay after hauling the LCGB 'Green Arrow Tour' on 3 July 1966. This picture was taken from the town bridge and illustrates the immense problems caused by parked cars. (Britton Collection)

The original station building at Weymouth was a wooden structure painted in the traditional British Railways Southern Region colour scheme. By the end of steam in July 1967 the stations looked a shabby reflection of bygone days. (Britton Collection)

20

LYMINGTON BRANCH

For the passenger, the journey down the Lymington branch began at Brockenhurst down bay platform. The two (and latterly three) coach trains always departed from Brockenhurst down bay platform, once the connecting train to Bournemouth or Weymouth had departed. When the driver had been given 'the tip' with a green flag and whistle from the guard, the train set off down the main line towards Lymington Junction signal box. As we accelerated away my eyes would focus on the carriage sidings and small turntable on the left-hand side. In the late 1950s to early 1960s it was possible to see a Drummond 700 or a Maunsell Q Class 0-6-0 shunting. On summer Saturdays, these old dependable workhorses would replace the Schools Class 4-4-0s, which brought in trains from Waterloo packed with tourists for the Isle of Wight. Weight restrictions precluded the Schools Class venturing down the branch and they would be turned on the 60ft turntable while the lighter 0-6-0 engine took the train onwards to Lymington Pier.

Lymington Junction was a magical place to watch main-line and branch activities, for at this point there was a three way junction. The main line to Bournemouth continued towards Sway, the 'Old Road' veered off with double track towards Homsley and Ringwood, while the Lymington branch swung off sharp left down the single line in front of the signal box. If one was picnicking, it was possible to walk under an arched bridge out into the open heath surrounded by New Forest ponies to observe the railway theatre. Alternatively, if your father knew the Lymington Junction signalman, it was possible to venture up into the box and witness things at first hand. On entering this busy box, the first things that struck me were the smell of polish, the lino floor, the almost constant sound of block bells and the occasional ring of a telephone with a message from one of the neighbouring signalmen. Within minutes of the down semi-fast passing hauled by a chattering Bulleid Light Pacific, the Lymington branch train entered the section from Brockenhurst. Our signalman descended the steps to place the single line token onto a special catcher device. The approaching two-coach train hauled by an Ivatt tank shut off, slowed to walking pace at the sharply curved junction, but once past, rapidly accelerated across the heathland to commence the 4½-mile journey.

From Lymington Junction there was a slight climb at first, before a descent down a 1 in 70 gradient. On the footplate the driver had the regulator open and speed was now building up to 40mph with the fireman just adding four to six shovelfuls of coal in the Union Jack firing method. We were now drifting along through the heather and trees towards Shirley Holmes halt, about 1½ miles from Lymington. Trains stopped here by request only during daylight hours, but our train trundled through with the safety valve gently lifting and a wisp of steam. Just over a mile ahead was a second unadvertised request halt, the Ampress Works Halt, which served the adjacent Wellworthy factory. Waiting to join our short train were two workers and the brakes were gently applied for us to gradually stop. Once the workers were aboard, we were smartly away and rapidly built up speed to head towards Lymington Town Station. On the approach our driver whistled up four long blasts on the Ivatt tank's Midland hooter, to warn the Lymington Town signalman of our approach and open the crossing gates for us to pass safely. On our left, after passing over the wooden gated crossing, was a small brick-built single road engine shed with a pitched slated roof, adjoining water tower and a small coal stage. Next was the small goods yard where another engine may have been lurking. In front of us on the right-hand side was the attractive Gothic-style brick-built station building with a train shed supported by cast-iron pillars on the opposite side.

As the train departed from Lymington Town Station the course of the line veered left and climbed over a picturesque 210ft eight-span iron viaduct, which crossed the estuary of Lymington Creek. This was a favourite location for photography with tourists and railway enthusiasts. The line from this point continued along an embankment and curved round passing the 1956-built signal box, over another level crossing before sweeping into Lymington Pier Station. In steam days the simple track layout comprised of a run-round loop with an engine release neck and buffer stops. Drivers of all engines had to proceed with extreme caution when running around their trains as one false move and it was a certain swim in the water! Waiting for incoming tourists transferring to the ferry for Yarmouth on the Isle of Wight was the paddle steamer *Freshwater* if one was lucky.

In the 1950s, it was possible to see ten branch trains on weekdays and six on Sundays. During the summer this was increased to twelve weekday and nine Sunday services. A word of caution, however, was that some of the train services were 'shorties' in that they operated only between the Pier and Town Stations or Brockenhurst to Lymington Town! The highlight of summer service operations were the through trains from Waterloo, which were hauled by Maunsell Q Class or Drummond 700 Class 0-6-0s. By the early 1960s, the winter timetable only provided for a sparse service down the Lymington branch and there was a gap of four and a half hours with no trains to Brockenhurst between 9.39 a.m. and 1.52 p.m.! For anyone heading to the West Wight on short, dark, cold winter days this was most off-putting.

One unusual common practice on the Lymington branch, unseen by the public but known to locals, was the routine of coaling branch engines en route! A small pile of coal would be deposited each morning in between the tracks of the shed coaling stage and the end of the platform at Lymington Town Station. On the return journey from Lymington Pier to Brockenhurst, the driver of the locomotive would carefully position his engine alongside the strategically positioned pile of coal. The fireman would quickly climb down and then shovel up enough coal onto the floor of the footplate to enable sufficient supplies for a further round trip. Perhaps the saddest thing I saw on the Lymington branch was on the last day of regular steam when all the engine tools, lamps, shed equipment and even the old spare M7 Westinghouse air brake pump were unceremoniously thrown out into the inspection pit. This would be a real treasure trove to a railway preservation society today. This once valuable kit was then all covered over with ash and may still be there buried to this day.

It was very sad but also great to see the visiting special enthusiast excursions in the last few years of steam. Who can forget the sight of the last Bulleid Q1 33006 coming down onto the branch with LCGB 'New Forester Rail Tour'? This was a really special occasion for all lovers of the Lymington branch. Well known railway photographers like A.E. 'Dusty' Durrant, John Courtney Haydon, the Reverend Canon Roger Lloyd and R.C. 'Dick' Riley gathered in homage at Lymington estuary to record the event on film. The Q1-hauled special doubled up to haul the combined special/branch service as it was necessary to cancel the regular timetabled passenger service. The heavily loaded train hauled by No. 33006 achieved a speed of 45mph heading down the branch, but found the tight curves very challenging and consequently arrived a few minutes down.

The final few weeks of steam operation on the Lymington branch were a depressing and desperate time for the staff. The branch was operated by two sets of men using two engines. When the branch freight services finished, coaling of engines ceased at Lymington Shed. Engines now arrived for turns of duty from Bournemouth Shed with their bunkers full to the top and often carrying a spare few choice lumps of coal on the footplate. Branch crews were constantly worrying as to whether their coal supply would see them through to the completion of their diagrammed duty. There were odd occasions when passing sympathetic Bournemouth-based crews even dropped off coal supplies from the tenders of their main-line Bulleid and Standard Class engines on the platform at Brockenhurst to help out their mates operating down the Lymington branch!

The final day of steam came on Sunday 2 April 1967, which was fittingly wet and miserable. From far and wide there suddenly appeared hundreds of railway enthusiasts to pay their last respects, suitably equipped with cameras, tripods, cine and tape recorders. Two Ivatt tanks, Nos 41320 and 41312, puled the last day's regular steam-hauled train services. It was not only time to say farewell to regular steam on the branch, but also to the two wonderful regular enginemen, driver Bert Farley and fireman Ray Glassey. Bert took redundancy while Ray transferred to Eastleigh. On that final steam-hauled train, the footplate was jam-packed with all sorts of friends and family members of the crew! Bert had a beaming smile as a well-wisher had presented him with a bottle of Johnny Walker scotch. As they departed from Lymington Pier there were cheers, whistles from No. 41312's hooter and explosions as the engine passed over a series of detonators on the line. A similar scene awaited this train at Lymington Town with crowds of well-wishers. As Ivatt tank No. 41312 entered the up loop platform at Brockenhurst, complete with a commemorative board proclaiming, 'The Last Steam Branch 1967', it was difficult to comprehend that it was really all over for steam on the Lymington branch. Even the headboard had a story behind it. Manufactured by the well-known Ron Cover of Eastleigh (famed for his tinplate smoke box door number plate), it had been painted with a red-coloured background. This caused complaints from official sources when placed on the branch engine operating services in the final week. The headboard was therefore hastily repainted overnight with a blue background and this appeased the protesters.

After taking water, Ivatt No. 41312 then finally set off from Brockenhurst for Eastleigh with the empty stock and thence on to her new home at Nine Elms with a replacement driver at the controls. Driver Frank Matthews, who took No. 41312 onwards, was a well-known character to railway enthusiasts and was nicknamed 'The Mad Monk'. Sure enough, Frank lived up to his name and blew the Ivatt tank hooter whistle for all he was worth as he headed over a few pre-planted detonators.

The 'Mad Monk' was still tooting away on No. 41312 in the darkness heading through the New Forest towards Woodfidley waking up the deer miles away. Back on the platform at Brockenhurst, the crowds cheered. Sorry, but my emotions did not allow me to join in the celebrations: 'What are they cheering for?' I thought, 'Life will never be the same without steam on the Lymington branch.'

Although the branch services were dieselised from the next day, Monday morning, pending full electrification, steam returned to the Lymington branch briefly the following Sunday on 9 April. There was a 'top and tail' LCGB railtour; 'the Hampshire Branch Lines Railtour' was topped by Standard Class 4 tank No. 80151 at the Lymington end and tailed by Ivatt 2 tank No. 41320 at the Brockenhurst end. Bulleid Light Pacific No. 34025 *Whimple* took the train on from Brockenhurst to Southampton for the return journey.

Lymington faces Yarmouth on the Isle of Wight, which was connected by railway-operated paddle steamers. The ferry link has today evolved into a modern and efficient car-ferry service operated by Wightlink. The town has a large tourist industry as it is on the doorstep of the New Forest and an attractive harbour. Lymington is a major yachting centre with three marinas.

Historically, Lymington began as an Anglo-Saxon village. The Jutes arrived from the Isle of Wight in the sixth century and founded a settlement called Limentun. The Old English word *tun* means a farm or hamlet, while *limen* means elm tree. The town is recorded in the Domesday Book of 1086 as 'Lentune'. In about AD 1200 the lord of the manor, William de Redvers, created New Lymington around what is now the Quay and High Street.

From the Middle Ages Lymington was famous for making traditional sea salt and this was refined along the Hurst Spit. The town has a rich tradition of smuggling and there are whispers that smugglers' tunnels run from the old inns to the town quay. The town centre is Georgian and Victorian with narrowed cobbled streets, providing an air of quaintness.

To many people, however, Lymington will always be known as the location of the last passenger-carrying steam-operated railway branch line in Britain.

M7 tank No. 30057 at Lymington Junction on 30 May 1963 at 11.02 a.m. with the 10.58 a.m. departure from Brockenhurst, arriving at Lymington Pier at 11.12 a.m. (Britton Collection)

Drummond M7 0-4-4 tank No. 30129 waits to depart Lymington Town Station with the 10.18 a.m. two-coach push-pull train to Lymington Pier on 1 June 1963. Note the waiting three-coach converted Maunsell push-pull set No. 611 waiting in the opposite direction, headed by M7 tank No. 30107. (Britton Collection)

Ivatt No. 41224 on 24 March 1967, departing from Lymington Town with the 4.58 p.m. to Lymington Pier. Note the red-coloured headboard, 'The Last Steam Branch 1967', which was later changed to blue. (Britton Collection)

This picture was taken on 24 March 1967, during the final week of regular steam-operated services on the Lymington branch. Ivatt No. 41312 is on the 4.25 p.m. service to Brockenhurst, which comprises two Bulleid coaches. (Britton Collection)

The preserved Ivatt Class 2 tank No. 41312, standing at the buffer stops at the end of Lymington Pier, looks as if she has seen better days. Behind her is the picturesque landscape of Lymington Harbour and the Isle of Wight. (David Peters)

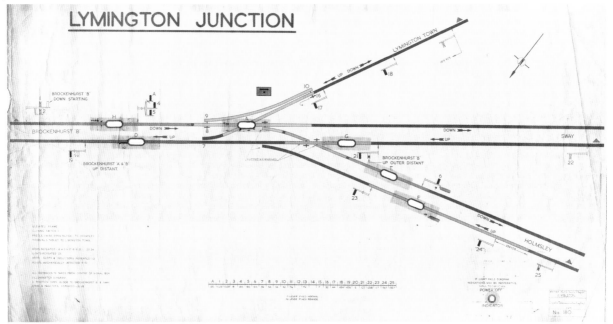

Drummond M7 No. 30254 is seen departing from Lymington Pier with the 7.20 a.m. local push-pull train to Brockenhurst on 31 May 1963. (Britton Collection)

21

SWANAGE BRANCH

The Swanage branch in the late 1950s and early 1960s was operated almost like a family business. Every member of the station staff, signalmen, train crews and P Way gang at Wareham, Corfe Castle and Swanage knew each other by sight and often by name. They all mucked in together to ensure that their railway branch was operated efficiently, for in those days there was much camaraderie and social interaction. For instance, the local P Way gang would deliver a pheasant or rabbit to a signalman and in return they would receive a bag of runner beans from the vegetable garden. Similarly passing loco crews would drop off lumps of coal at P Way huts during the winter months to ensure that the linesmen kept warm. The railway staff were very tolerant to photographers and railway enthusiasts and to regulars they were very welcoming. The branch had its own set of drivers, Jock Hapgood and Jack Spicer, who always extended an open invitation to their engine footplates. Local Swanage guard Alec Dudley was similarly very welcoming to visitors and would show those who were interested what was required to be a guard. For me, this included the thrill of blowing the guard's whistle and waving the green flag at train departure!

The 11¼-mile branch from Wareham to Swanage was opened in May 1885. It left the main Bournemouth–Weymouth line approximately 1 mile west of Wareham and 126 miles from Waterloo at Worgret Junction. Passengers wishing to travel to Corfe Castle or Swanage joined at Wareham Bay platform. On summer Saturdays the branch came into its own, with through trains to and from Waterloo crammed with holidaymakers and day trippers. These through trains hauled by Bulleid Light Pacifics brought variety and excitement to the line. The backbone of the services was the Bournemouth-based Drummond M7s, hauling two-coach push-pull sets. The last M7-hauled train ran on Saturday 9 May 1964, hauled by No. 30107. They were initially augmented by BR Class 3 tanks but Ivatt 2-6-2 and BR Standard Class 4 2-6-4 tanks became the replacement motive power for local services. Other regular motive power to be seen on the local daily goods services were Drummond 700s, Maunsell Q Class and BR Standard 76xxx moguls. On occasion it was also possible to see Maunsell U Class moguls and BR Standard 4 75xxx Class hauling passenger services from Bournemouth, Eastleigh and Salisbury.

The Bournemouth-based push-pull fitted M7s were always very popular with Swanage footplate crews, so long as they were maintained well with cleaned tubes. The M7s were unofficially named by railway staff: No. 30052 was christened 'Lord Elgin', No. 30108 was known as 'Rosie' and No. 30111 'Lord Nelson'. Such was the affection for No. 30108 that at one time she even had a rose painted below her number! In the last few months of service, in late 1963 and early 1964, the surviving run down M7s began to show their years and all too often with bad time-keeping and frequent failures in traffic, only to be hastily replaced by a Q Class shunting at Hamworthy. For some of the veteran Swanage-based drivers, like Jack Spicer and Jock Hapgood, the transition from M7s to more modern steam traction was difficult to accept. The two initial replacement BR Standard 3s Nos 82026 and 82028 were revolutionary, moving from the Victorian era to the twentieth century with their spacious cabs, screw reversers, steam brakes, drop grates and speedometers. The BR Standard 3 tanks were soon replaced by their larger sisters, the BR Standard 4 80xxx tanks and Ivatt 2 tanks. The popular opinion among branch crews was that the Standard 4 tanks, although smooth and powerful, consumed more coal than the Ivatt 2-6-2 tanks. With their 4ft grates, the Ivatts were considered to be more economical, light and responsive. The ideal Ivatt tank would only take one 1,350-gallon tankful of water for a return journey from Wareham to Swanage. The only disadvantage was they were not push-pull fitted, resulting in stock having to be run around at both ends of the journey plus coupling and uncoupling. Nevertheless, they became very popular with Swanage crews.

Regular passenger steam services came to an end on the Swanage branch on Sunday 4 September 1966 with Standard Class 4 76010 hauling the branch's two-Bulleid-coach set on the local service and Standard 4 tank 80140 covering the 6.12 p.m. Swanage–Eastleigh stopping train.

The passenger carriage stock on the branch was always a pleasure to travel in and was made up of non-corridor two-coach sets with droplight windows and leather straps. In the summer of 1960 one of the few remaining ex-LSWR gate sets made an appearance on the branch and was quite smooth and comfortable to travel in. At the same time, converted push-pull Maunsell corridor stock entered service on the branch. In the latter years Bulleid stock in turn replaced the push-pull sets prior to dieselisation in 1966. The variety of through carriage stock from Waterloo and inter-regional workings was always of great interest. I have witnessed stock based at Swanage from Western Region Hawkesworth and Collett carriages to Eastern Region Gresley coaches. Rakes of Bulleid stock from Waterloo were the norm and would remain berthed in the Swanage sidings for days on end.

When visiting Corfe Castle, there was a major source of interest for the carriage enthusiast with camping coaches. Prior to 1960, there was an ex-LSWR brake third No. 2753, but this was replaced by the Pullman car *Coral*, which had been converted especially for use as a camping coach. Such was the popularity of this Pullman that a second, *Milan*, joined it the following year. These two Pullmans became a great source of interest to visitors and enthusiasts. Sadly, these two delightful carriages were broken up in 1968, which, in hindsight was a massive mistake.

By the 1960s regular freight traffic was in serious decline. The two local goods trains, usually hauled by Dummond 700, Maunsell Q or BR Standard 4 Class, dropped to two per week. The Furzebrook clay traffic also decreased, but continued to be steam hauled up to the end of regular SR steam in 1967.

A return trip down the Swanage branch was always a great occasion for the passenger. Leaving the down bay platform at Wareham, our two-coach train would rapidly accelerate, heading up the main line towards Worgret Junction. As we approached Worgret the line passed under the A352 Wareham to Wool main road. At this point our train slowed rapidly to walking pace and for the railway enthusiast it was eyes right, out of the carriage window, to observe the token exchange as the driver collected the leather pouch containing the single line token for the section ahead to Corfe Castle. At this point the line swung left in a sharp curve in a cutting and under a small farmer's occupation bridge. Once out onto the long straight, our train would build up speed again on the descent towards the viaduct, crossing the River Frome ready for the climb up to Holme Lane Bridge and through the woods to Grange Road overbridge. This was a great place to encounter local wildlife as deer and pheasants would frequently dart in front of the approaching trains. As we climbed towards Furzebrook, our engine would be working hard and trying to maintain a speed of 35 to 40mph.

Once past the Furzebrook clay sidings, our train headed down the straight towards Montella. Beyond here BR severed the link to Swanage in 1972. During the summer months this section would be a favourite basking ground for adders, lizards and slow worms. The line then swept under the brick-built Catseye Bridge that carried the A351 road before descending down the gradient through Woodpecker Cutting towards Eldon's Siding. This was once the interchange point for the narrow-gauge workings to collect ball clay.

After sweeping through Norden Cutting, passengers had a clear view of the 'Gateway to the Purbecks – Corfe Castle'. Trains would whistle at this point, engines shut off and the brakes would be gradually applied as they passed over the impressive stone viaduct crossing the River Corfe and the B3351 Studland road, before sweeping into the short cutting. To the left of the carriage window passengers could gaze up the steep slopes of the East Hill, while on the opposite side there was a good view across the Corfe Castle village rooftops.

Arriving at Corfe Castle Station was a wonderful experience. Stepping out onto the platform, the scene was dominated by the castle ruins. This small rural Southern Station was the intermediate crossing point on the branch where branch trains could pass. The station building on the up platform was constructed from Purbeck stone with a canopy, oil lamps and an end-loading dock. Corfe was equipped with a goods shed and an ornate valance, which sheltered loading vehicles. In the station yard there was the coal yard operated by L.G. Stockley, which was extremely busy and regularly shunted daily by a Maunsell Q Class or Drummond 700.

The castle was built by William the Conqueror and dates back to the eleventh century. Strategically it commands a gap in the Purbeck Hills. In 1572 Corfe Castle was sold by Elizabeth I to Sir Christopher Hatton and passed into the hands of Sir John Bankes in 1635. During the English Civil War Sir John's wife, Lady Mary Bankes, led the defence of the castle twice when besieged by Parliamentary forces. The first siege in 1643 was unsuccessful but the castle fell in 1645. The Parliamentary commander, Colonel Bingham, colluded with one of the castle garrison's officers, Colonel Pitman. He proposed that he should go to Somerset and return with 100 Royalist reinforcements. However, the troops that entered Corfe Castle were Parliamentarians in disguise. Once within the walls, they waited until there was a Parliamentary attack before making a move. The Royalist defenders were simultaneously attacked from without and within, the portcullis was raised and the castle fell. In March 1645 the castle was demolished under the orders of Oliver Cromwell and the ruins are now owned by the National Trust.

Departing from Corfe Castle past the home signal, down trains now tackled the 1 in 80 climb. With a heavy train this was sometimes a challenge for a light-footed Bulleid West Country Pacific. The train now headed across Corfe Common before sweeping around the curve to Afflington Road Bridge. Continuing the climb through a cutting the line then began to descend past Woodyhyde to Haycraft's Lane Bridge (the site of the Swanage Railway's Harman's Cross Station). From now on it was downhill most of the way to Swanage at a speed of up to 45mph past Quarr Farm, the woods of the Wilderness, under Valley Road Nursery Bridge, New Barn and Herston. Heading into the outskirts of Swanage, the railway enthusiast would look out on the left-hand side after passing King George's Playing Field to see what engines were in the small one-road shed or on the turntable. Immediately after passing under Northbrook Road Bridge, the attention of the enthusiast would switch to the right-hand side of the train to observe what was waiting in the station yard and goods yard. Quite often the station yard sidings would contain a set of coaches ready to return to the Midlands the following Saturday and if you were lucky a Q or 700 Class could be spotted shunting the branch freight.

After arriving at Swanage, 136 miles from Waterloo, there was always a hive of activity while passengers got off the train and the locomotive ran around the carriage stock unless it was push-pull operated. In the 1950s and '60s, my late father would make for the 1884-built signal box to meet up with Signalman Arthur Galton or Signalman Jimmy Hunt. The Swanage signalmen were always so welcoming to visitors wishing to view the twenty-three-lever frame. With no one around, my father would be invited to unofficially have a go at operating the box under careful instruction of Signalman Galton. Everything would be straightforward until he came to pull off lever number 2, which operated the down home signal which was some way from the box. After several attempts my father would give up. Arthur Galton would then expertly take over and show how it was done with ease – one quick all in one pull. Inside Swanage signal box it was cosy, but it could be freezing cold in the winter and boiling hot in the summer months. The lasting memory of the box was that it was maintained in pristine condition until the day it closed on Tuesday 6 June 1967.

During the Second World War the branch was not the sole preserve of M7-operated push-pull trains. One morning a special arrived hauled by two LMS 4Fs originating from the Somerset & Dorset line. Their unadvertised train consisted of rail-mounted guns which were positioned at Eldon sidings. On another occasion a VIP train arrived on the branch with army generals and smartly dressed officials in suits on board. It was hauled by an LNER B12 locomotive! Prior to D-Day in 1944, the Swanage branch was crammed full of American GI troops. To local children they were an answer to prayer as they would scrounge chocolate and cookies and they were introduced to American chewing gum from their 'K ration' box on Swanage platform. There are stories of special troop trains carrying support equipment, such as Jeeps and lorries, arriving behind former LSWR Jumbos and 700 Class engines, congesting the Swanage yard. During the war there were three extra trains each day working from Swanage to Holton Heath to convey workers to the Royal Ordinance factory where shells were made. As the local men were away fighting for their country, the commuters on the train were mostly women. The locally based American GIs used to refer to these trains as 'Glamour Puffers' and wolf whistle as they arrived and departed at Swanage, Corfe Castle and Wareham. Accounts related that on occasions there were some passionate platform scenes between GIs and local girls, which were totally disapproved of by the locals.

Just after the war, LMS 2P and 4F locomotives being turned and serviced at Swanage Shed. On enquiring with the footplate crews they related that the engines had come from Templecombe off the S&D and were at Swanage to drop off pigeons with van trains from Huddersfield and Manchester. One morning the Swanage signalman tipped off local railway enthusiasts about an unusual working, a Western Region 43xx that had worked in via Dorchester West on an excursion train. The driver curtly related that Western Region engines had historically always had running rights as far as Corfe Castle from Dorchester in return for the Southern having running rights from Dorchester to Weymouth over his Western lines. (This special Western Region working was also reported in the railway press at the time.)

Perhaps the most amusing sight ever witnessed at Swanage Station occurred one Tuesday morning in April 1964. Drummond M7 tank No. 30107 which was patiently waiting in the bay platform with the branch train for Wareham was by this time in her last few weeks of Swanage branch service and was leaking steam and looked as if she had seen better days. Out of the corner of our eye we spotted a local farmer entering onto the platform via the side of the station entrance with his prize ram ready to be loaded for Dorchester market into the luggage compartment of the Maunsell brake at the end of the platform. While in the process of loading the ram assisted by the guard Alec Dudley, the woolly animal had other ideas and suddenly broke loose from his rope tether. The determined ram sprinted off down the platform, scattering bemused waiting passengers and dodging porters' platform trolleys. It took some minutes to recapture the poor ram, which was cornered at the other end of the platform opposite the Railway Hotel by exhausted driver Jock Hapgood, guard Alec Dudley, porter Taffy Hazell and the farmer. All four marched the protesting baaing prisoner in close escort to the train where he was securely tied to a corner of the luggage compartment in disgrace. With the job completed, the waiting passengers on the branch train who had been observing the commotion burst out in a round of spontaneous applause!

In the final years of steam on the Swanage branch, several enthusiast specials visited. On 25 March 1967, the Manchester Rail Travel Society ran the 'Hants & Dorset Branch Flyer', from Southampton Central. The Ivatt tank No. 41320 hauled the special onto the Swanage branch. This special was followed on Sunday 7 May 1967 when the LCGB ran two 'Dorset Coast Express' top and tail trips down the branch. The morning run ran with un-rebuilt 34023 *Blackmore Vale* at the Swanage end and Standard 4MT No. 76026 at the Wareham end. In the afternoon, Standard 4 tank No. 80011 was substituted at the Wareham end. A few weeks later, on a sunny day, the Warwickshire Railway Society ran their 'Farewell to Steam on the LSWR' tour from Birmingham New Street. On this occasion Bulleid rebuilt West Country No. 34004 *Yeovil* hauled the train with Standard 4 tank No. 80146 at the rear of the train. The last BR passenger working was the RCTS 'Farewell to Southern Steam' Rail Tour originating from Waterloo on 18 June 1967. Working rebuilt Bulleid Battle of Britain No. 34089 *602 Squadron* hauled the train into Swanage with Standard tank 80146 at the Wareham end. Many enthusiasts and spectators flocked to the lineside and bridges to watch the pair whistle their sad farewells as they departed from Swanage.

Steam did venture onto the branch as far as Furzebrook Clay sidings until almost the end. Many enthusiasts have stated that No. 34025 *Whimple* was the last BR steam locomotive on the Swanage branch on 30 June 1967. However the honour fell to No. 34021 *Dartmoor* hauling the very last BR clay steam working on the morning of Friday 7 July 1967. Word soon spread, and *Dartmoor* was watched by a small gathering of locals at Furzebrook sidings, Holme Lane Bridge and Wareham. *Dartmoor* went on to haul the late afternoon Bournemouth–Eastleigh train which was packed with enthusiasts.

The town is first mentioned in historical texts in the *Anglo-Saxon Chronicle* of AD 877, where it is stated as being the scene of a great naval victory by King Alfred over the Danes. A column commemorates this on the seafront at Swanage. Today the town has developed into a popular resort on the Jurassic Coast and is the home of the Swanage Railway.

A dad in his summer shorts is busy jotting down the number of a passing Waterloo express, while his son watches the crew of the Swanage branch train stroll down the platform at Wareham. Ivatt 2 tank No. 41230 is left to simmer in the bay platform at the head of the 5.01 p.m departure for Swanage on 20 August 1966. (Britton Collection)

The 4.03 p.m. Swanage–Wareham train, headed by BR Standard 4 2-6-0 No. 76010, is seen passing Blue Pool at Furzebrook on Sunday 4 September 1966. This was the last day of steam operation on branch services. (Britton Collection)

Viewed from the castle mound at Corfe Castle, an Ivatt tank is seen hauling the two-coach Bulleid branch train across the handsome Purbeck stone-built Corfe Viaduct towards Wareham on 5 August 1965. Beneath are queues of frustrated cars waiting on the B3351 Studland road: some things never change. (Britton Collection)

Approaching the dramatic ruins of Corfe Castle is Ivatt Class 2 tank No. 41275 with a train for Swanage on 7 September 1965. (Bryan Hicks)

Ivatt Class 2 tank No. 41316 rattles along Corfe Common towards Harmans Cross and Swanage on 7 September 1965. The cows appear to be used to this hourly occurrence. (Bryan Hicks)

The attractive twety-three-lever-frame Swanage signal box, which was built in 1884, is seen on 7 May 1967. (Britton Collection)

Ivatt tanks Nos 41284 and 41301, heading the LCGB 'Dorset Belle Rail Tour' on 27 February 1966, prepare to return to Wareham. (Britton Collection)

Preserved Ivatt 2-6-2 tank No. 41312 simmers gently in the bay platform at Swanage on 20 August 1965. (Britton Collection)

The regulator is opened and un-rebuilt Bulleid West Country No. 4023 *Blackmore Vale* climbs away from Corfe Castle to Swanage with the LCGB's 'Dorset Coast Express Tour' on 7 May 1967. (Britton Collection)

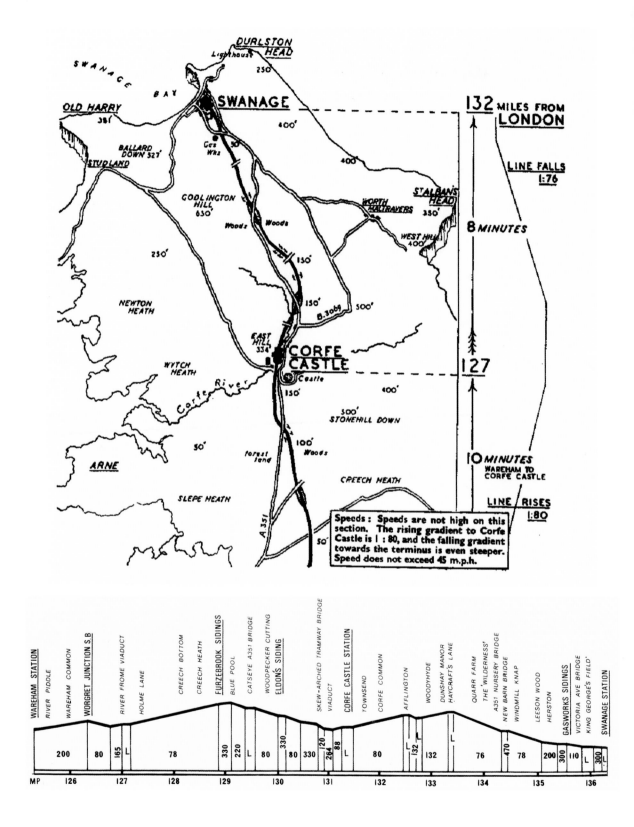